AF856295

The Non–Trials

as lived by

Julian Heicklen

by Julian Heicklen

A true story of trials that did not occur inspired by "The Trial," by Franz Kafka, which was a fictional story of a trial that did occur.

Published January, 2011 by
Ishi Press in New York and Tokyo

Copyright © 2011 by Julian Heicklen

All rights reserved according to International Law. No Part of this book may be reproduced by anyone for public or private use without the written permission of the publisher.

ISBN 4–87187–900–3
978–4–87187–900–2

Ishi Press International
1664 Davidson Avenue, Suite 1B
Bronx NY 10453–7877 USA
1–917–507–7226

Printed in the United States of America

Dedicated to the U. S. Constitution. May it be resurrected.

The law is the whore of government. The courts are its pimps. The law was meant to protect persons and property. Instead it is used to seduce us into enslavement.

"THE PRICE OF LIBERTY IS ETERNAL VIGILANCE"
Wendell Phillips

"THE PRICE OF JUSTICE IS ETERNAL PUBLICITY"
author unknown

ACKNOWLEDGMENTS

The author thanks the following for providing the material which inspired the writing of this book:

New York City Police
New York City Department of Corrections
New York City District Attorney
New York City Comptroller's Office
Criminal Court of Manhattan
NY State Supreme Court: Civil Division2
NY Supreme Court: Appellate Division
U. S. District Court: Southern District of New York
U. S. Court of Appeals: Second Circuit2

ABOUT THE AUTHOR

Julian Heicklen has been married to the former Susan Hook since 1959. They have 3 daughters and 8 grandchildren.

Julian Heicklen was born at an early age. At 8 days he was circumcised. He found this to be so traumatic, that he did not walk or talk for one year.

There was nothing unusual about his childhood. After graduating from high school, he went to Cornell University to become an engineering nerd. Unfortunately while in high school his uncle had bought a book about the U. S. Constitution and Declaration of Independence for him. To complicate matters he read Les Miserables by Victor Hugo and The Fountainhead by Ayn Rand while at Cornell.

As a result he was transformed from an engineering nerd into a freedom maniac. His behavior became socially unacceptable. He stole a house, won the Yom Kippur war for Israel, carried on a correspondence with Soviet Premier Yuri Andropov, tried to sue the U. S. Post Office, smoked marijuana every Thursday at noon for three years in front of the main gate of Penn State University and the Centre County Courthouse. He had the State College noise ordinance declared unconstitutional, and he has been arrested 29 times and incarcerated 9 times.

His wife and daughters want to commit him to an old age home. However he prefers to go to prison where he gets free room, board, and medical care. In addition he gets health club for 1 hour a day and something he could never afford—around the clock police protection. Besides, the people in the prison are more interesting than those in the old age home.

A more conventional biography follows:

Academic Career

Julian Heicklen was born and raised in Rochester, NY. He attended Martin B. Anderson grammar school Number 1, where he was chosen for academic excellence to be standard bearer of the American flag.

He attended Monroe High School, where he was a member of the Honor Society, President of Adelphians, and winner of the Bausch & Lomb Award for excellence in science.

From 1949–1954, he attended Cornell University with the aid of New York State Regents and McMullen scholarships. In

1954, he started graduate studies as a National Science Fellow at the University of Rochester. In 1958, he received a Ph.D in chemistry. Then followed postdoctoral fellowships at the University of Rochester, the University of Minnesota, and the University of California at Berkeley.

From 1962-1967, he was employed by the Aerospace Corporation in El Segundo, CA, where he became a section head. In 1967 he joined the Chemistry Department at Penn State University as an associate professor, was promoted to Professor in 1971, and retired as Emeritus Professor of Chemistry at the end of 1991. At Penn State, he was affiliated with the Center for Air Environment Studies, the Ionosphere Research Laboratory, and the Institute for Biological Sciences.

He is the author of two books: " Atmospheric Chemistry" and "Colloid Formation and Growth." He coauthored 27 scientific review articles and 257 research papers in chemistry and related fields. Though he is not a lawyer, he has tried or been involved in over 40 legal cases in PA, NY, NJ, and U. S. federal courts. In addition he has authored four reports on crime and drugs and seven pamphlets on contract bridge.

As a result of his professional work, he was on the Editorial board of the Journal of Photochemistry (1972–89). He was a Fellow of the American Physical Society, the NY Academy of Sciences, and the American Association for the Advancement of Science. He won the American Chemical Society Award for Creative Advances in Environmental Sciences and Technology (1984); the Boris Pregel Award for Applied Science and Technology of the New York Academy of Sciences (1984); and the Frank A. Chambers Award of the Air Pollution Control Association (1985).

Civil Rights Activities

Julian Heicklen is a well-known, if not widely known, civil rights activist. He has been arrested 29 times in civil rights demonstrations and incarcerated 9 times. As a result of one of his arrests, the State College, PA noise ordinance was declared unconstitutional. He sued the Boro of State College and received $8000.00 in an out-of-court settlement.

He was the Libertarian Party candidate for attorney general of Pennsylvania in 2000. He was the recipient of the Pennsylvania Libertarian Party "Achievement Award" in 1999 and again in 2006. He was awarded the Todah Award of the Jewish Congregation at Rockview Prison in 1995.

"The Non-Trials" is the story of his journey through the NY state and U. S. federal courts as a result of his arrest on April 17, 2007, while demonstrating against Iranian President Mahmoud Ahmadinejad across the street from the UN building in New York City.

In his senior year in high school, he was President of the Upstate New York Region of Senior Judea (the high-school arm of the Zionist Organization of America).

Julian Heicklen was Action Chairman for the Los Angeles chapter of the Congress of Racial Equality (CORE) in 1962–63. In 1962 he invented and executed the first "dwell-in" in which CORE seized a home for a black family in a housing tract in Wilmington, CA. As a result, a court **ORDER** was issued which ended housing discrimination in California based on race, religion, or country of national origin. Julian Heicklen is a Founding sponsor of the Martin Luther King, Jr. National Memorial.

He held several official positions for the Centre County of PA chapter of ACLU (1969–1980). He was National Coordinator of the Small Committees of the Committee on the International Freedom of Scientists of the American Physical Society (1983–86), and a Member of the National Board of Directors of the Committee of Concerned Scientists (1987–2004). He founded the organization Smart on Crime and was its Executive Director (1996–2006). Also he was the Pennsylvania representative for the Fully Informed Jury Association (2000–2006).

He was an official visitor for the Pennsylvania Prison Society (1996), a staff member of CentrePeace (1996), a mentor for Project Change of Centre County, PA (1996), an area coordinator for the Justice Fellowship Task Force (1996–97), and a prison reporter for Voices of Central Pennsylvania (1997).

He was on the Board of Directors of the Tri-State (PA, NJ, DE) Drug Policy Forum (2001–03) and the Pennsylvania chapter of NORML (2001–03), a co-sponsor of the Million Marijuana Marches (1999–2003), and High Times Magazine Freedom Fighter of the Month (May 1998).

He was the organizer and Chair, Centre County, PA Chapter of the Libertarian Party (1997); a member of the Libertarian Party of Pennsylvania Board of Directors (1998-2002); Student Outreach Program Chairman (1999- 2002); Western Vice Chair. Libertarian Party of PA (2002); Faculty Advisor, College Libertarians of Penn State (1998-2001). He served on the Libertarian Party National Platform Committee (2002).

In 2009, he organized "Tyranny Fighters" to restore the Bill of Rights in the U. S. Constitution. In 2010, he founded Tyranny Fighters web radio show on LWRN. In 2010 he was awarded the Handcuff Award at the Porcupine Festival for multiple arrests in the cause of freedom.

Civic Activities

Julian Heicklen was an active member of Congregation Brit Shalom in State College, PA. He served on many committees and terms as Treasurer and Vice President. He was active in outreach programs and spoke about Judaism at several Christian churches.

For the extended Jewish community of Centre County, PA, he was Head of the Cemetery Committee and Chair of the mens'

Hevra Kadisha (committee which prepares bodies for burial), both for over 30 years. One year he and his wife were co-chairs of the annual United Jewish Appeal dinner.

He also delivered lunches to the home-bound for Meals on Wheels.

FORWARD

I was kidnapped on April 17, 2007, by New York City police and incarcerated for 22 hours. A bench warrant was issued for my arrest on June 20, 2007, and I was a fugitive from justice in New York State until my arrest on May 25, 2010.

I have submitted pleadings with three New York state courts and two U. S. federal courts. In addition to time spent preparing documents, costs have included manuscript preparation and reproduction, mailing costs, fees paid to the courts and fees for service of summons.

The police stole two picket signs from me, whose replacement cost was $96.30, and the Criminal Court of Manhattan stole $210 from me (returned 3 years later). There were filing fees of $305 with New York Supreme Court: Civil Division, $45 with the New York State Supreme Court: Appellate Division, $1610 (two $350 filing fees and two $455 fees for the Notice of Appeal) with the U. S. District Court for the Southern District of New York, and $450 with the U. S. Court of Appeals: Second Circuit for the Petition for a Writ of Mandamus.

Copies of all pertinent documents that I submitted to the courts can be found on my web page at: http://www.personal.psu.edu/faculty/j/p/jph13/NY_City_Lawsuit_Links.html and http://www.personal.psu.edu/faculty/j/p/jph13/Judicial_Failure.html. This book is a summary of those events.

As a result of these and other incidents, Tyranny Fighters was born. All of this happened because I stood on a sidewalk in Manhattan holding signs that read:

STOP HATING JEWS

CONTENTS

I. PROLOGUE

Why have I written this book? Because I love my country as it should be, but it no longer is. I am ashamed of my country, deeply ashamed, as only one can be who expected better.

The government of the United States is the best ever imagined. It was organized to serve the people without enslaving them. Abraham Lincoln correctly called it "The last best hope of mankind." It is a constitutional republic with four tiers of government: municipal, county, state, and federal. Both the state and federal governments have constitutions as the ultimate authority to protect the minority from the tyranny of the majority. They each have three branches of government: legislative, executive, and judicial, to check on each other's potential excesses. In addition there is a free press to act as the fourth estate and expose any misdeeds. Finally, every individual is protected from unjust incarceration by a jury of 12 peers, who must agree unanimously to find guilt.

A. THE PRISON STATE

The United States proudly proclaims itself as the land of the free, but it is not true. The United States is the number one prison state in the world. With 4.54 percent of the world's population, it has 25 percent of the world's prisoners. The United States has about the same number of prisoners as China and Russia (the number 2 and 3 prison states) combined. These two countries combined have almost 4.8 times the population of the United States.

According to the New York Times of April 23, 2008 (page A1), The United states has 2.3 million criminals behind bars. About one in every one hundred adults in the United States was in prison in April, 2008. Since a vast majority of these are men, 2.27% of males over the age of 14 years are prisoners. For ages between 20 and 34, 1 in 30 men is behind bars. For black men over 14 years old, 13.6% were behind bars at the end of 2008 according to U. S. Justice Department statistics. There were 7.3 million adults in prison, on probation, or parole (1 in 31 adults) at the end of 2007 in the United States.

This does not include the more than 300,000 illegal immigrants held in detention camps each year. According to an editorial in the New York Times (August 1, 2009, p. A16), "detainees were locked up and forgotten. They were denied access to lawyers and their families. They languished , sickened and died without medical attention." In a detention center in rural Bisile, LA, immigrants "have pleaded for access to medicine, lawyers, their families, and basic information about their cases. They lack underwear and soap. Rats, spiders, flies and filth are rampant."

In the United states 1.6 million children have a parent in prison. They do not have a stable family life, which leads to disruptive behavior and failure in school. A significant fraction of the so-called criminals are under government supervision for owning a vegetable (marijuana), a fungus (mushrooms), a plant (cocaine), or a flower (heroin). According to a Marijuana Policy Project letter of October, 2008, for marijuana alone there were 872,720 arrests in 2007, more than for all the violent crimes combined. Meanwhile a child legally can enter a neighborhood store and purchase rat poison.

Black males particularly are punished. For Black male adults, about one in eleven currently are in prison. On the streets of our cities and towns, about one in six Black adult men are on parole or probation. One-third of all Black males will be felons (that is right: felons) during their lifetimes. Black people commit "crimes" at about 4 times the rate of white people. Yet they are incarcerated at about 8 times the rate. Racism is still rampant in the United States. "Crimes" are in quotes, because many of them should not be crimes at all.

Treatment of prisoners can be cruel. A significant contributor to the problem is overcrowding. There are not enough cells to accommodate all prisoners adequately. Often they share cells and fear their cellmate. When the author was associated with The Pennsylvania Prison Society and Smart on Crime (1996–2004), he was in contact with about 200 inmates in the Pennsylvania state prisons (euphemistically called State Correctional Institutions). Some of their unpleasant experiences are summarized on my web page at : http://www.personal.psu.edu/faculty/j/p/jph13/TalesfromPAPrisons.html. Conditions in many other state prisons, particularly in the South, are even worse.

On May 21, 2008, Nicholas Kristoff reported in the New York Times Sunday Opinion section that Sami al-Hajj, a cameraman for Al Jazeera, was released from Guantanamo prison after being held without charges for six years. Mr. Hajj alleged that he was beaten and punished for a hunger strike by having feeding tubes forcibly inserted into his nose and throat without lubricant. Prisoners at Guantanamo are not allowed to see their families. Mr. Hajj had not seen his 7-year old son since he was a baby.

Kristoff further reported that Murat Kurnaz, a prisoner in Guantanamo for nearly 5 years, described prolonged torture that included interruptions by a doctor to ensure that he was well enough for the torture to continue.

Mahvish Rukhsana Khan described a pediatrician who was beaten, doused with ice water, and paraded around naked. After 3 years, it was decided that he was innocent and sent home. Torture was routine. That is why more than 100 prisoners have died in American custody in Afghanistan, Iraq, and Guantanamo.

B. GOVERNMENT ABUSES

The executive branch of the federal government under President George W. Bush lied to us about weapons of mass destruction in Iraq. This led to a war both costly in lives and money. He engaged in illegal wiretapping, discarded the U. S. Constitutional right to *habeas corpus*, imprisoned people without a trial, and permitted (encouraged) torture of prisoners. Two of his U. S. attorney generals (Alberto Gonzales and Michael B. Mukasey) declared torture by the government to be legal. The torture methods included keeping detainees awake for 11 straight days or placing them in a dark, cramped box. Sometimes insects were put in the box to exploit their fears. According to the New York Times front page story of April 20, 2009, Abu Zubaydah was waterboarded 183 times in March 2003.

Vice President Cheney and his assistant, Scooter Libby, exposed an undercover CIA agent, which is a federal crime. Scooter Libby was sentenced to prison, but did not serve, because President Bush commuted the prison term punishment.

President Barak Obama's Secretary of the Treasury, Timothy Geithner, admitted that he had failed to pay tens of thousands of dollars in federal self- employment taxes while working for the International Monetary Fund despite having signed paperwork acknowledging the obligation.

Former presidents were also guilty of crimes. President Clinton was a proliferate philanderer. He was found guilty of perjury. As a result, he was impeached by the House of Representatives, but not convicted by the Senate.

President George H. W. Bush libeled Michael Dukakis, his opponent in the 1988 presidential election, by insinuating that he was responsible for crimes committed by Willie Horton.

The Reagan administration engaged in illegal arms sales between Iran and central American forces (the Iran-Contra affair). President Reagan was spared criminal involvement, because he claimed he had no knowledge of the affair. However his national security advisor, Robert McFarlane pleaded guilty in 1988 to four counts of withholding information from Congress for his role in the Iran-Contra cover-up. He was sentenced to two years' probation and a $20,000 fine but was pardoned by President George H. W. Bush in the waning hours of his presidency on Christmas Eve 1992 along with the other key players in the scandal.

Lieutenant Colonel Oliver North was tried in 1988 in relation to his activities while at the National Security Council. He was indicted on sixteen felony counts and on May 4, 1989, he was initially convicted of three: accepting an illegal gratuity, aiding and abetting in the obstruction of a congressional inquiry, and destruction of documents (by his secretary, Fawn Hall, on his instructions). He was sentenced by U. S. District Judge Gerhard A. Gesell on July 5, 1989, to a three-year suspended prison term, two years probation, $150,000 in fines, and 1,200 hours community service. However, on July 20, 1990, with the help of the American Civil Liberties Union (ACLU), North's convictions were vacated, after the appeals court found that witnesses in his trial might have been impermissibly affected by his immunized congressional testimony.

President Richard Nixon ran a major crime syndicate from the oval office in the White House. His top three advisors, H. R. Haldeman, John Erlichman, and Charles Colson, as well as other underlings, were sent to prison. President Nixon only escaped prison, because his successor, Gerald Ford, granted him a pardon. L. Patrick Gray, the Head of the FBI, destroyed incriminating evidence against Richard Nixon by dumping it into the Potomac River.

Nixon's vice president, Spiro Agnew was taking illegal financial gifts while in office. Agnew's attorneys entered into plea bargaining with the federal prosecutors. In return for pleading *nolo contendere*, or no contest, to the tax charge and paying $160,000 in back taxes (with the help of a loan from Frank Sinatra), he would receive a suspended sentence and a $10,000 fine. On October 10,

1973, while Spiro T. Agnew appeared in federal court in Baltimore, he resigned the vice presidency.

U. S. Supreme Court Justice Clarence Thomas made improper (a euphemism for disgusting) sexual advances to his female employees, notably Anita Hill. Chief Justice of the U. S. Supreme Court Abe Fortas had a conflict of interest and resigned from the Court.

The U. S. Congress is a hotbed of criminal activity.

The Keating Five were five United States Senators accused of corruption in 1989, igniting a major political scandal as part of the larger savings and loan crisis of the late 1980s and early 1990s. The five senators, Alan Cranston (D, CA), Dennis DeConcini (D, AZ), John Glenn (D, OH), John McCain (R, AZ), and Donald W. Riegle (D, MI), were accused of improperly intervening in 1987 on behalf of Charles H. Keating, Jr., Chairman of the Lincoln Savings and Loan Association, which was the target of a regulatory investigation by the Federal Home Loan Bank Board (FHLBB). The FHLBB subsequently backed off taking action against Lincoln.

Lincoln Savings and Loan collapsed in 1989, at a cost of over $3 billion to the federal government. Some 23,000 Lincoln bondholders were defrauded and many elderly investors lost their life savings. The substantial political contributions that Keating had made to each of the senators, totaling $1.3 million, attracted considerable public and media attention.

After a lengthy investigation, the Senate Ethics Committee determined in 1991 that Alan Cranston, Dennis DeConcini, and Donald Riegle had substantially and improperly interfered with the FHLBB in its investigation of Lincoln Savings, with Cranston receiving a formal reprimand. Senators John Glenn and John McCain were cleared of having acted improperly but were criticized for having exercised "poor judgment." All five of the senators involved served out their senate terms. Only Glenn and McCain ran for reelection, and they both succeeded. McCain would go on to become the Republican nominee for president in 2008. (http://en.wikipedia.org/wiki/Keating_Five).

Senator Ted Stevens (R, AK) was convicted for corruption charges in October, 2008. In an indictment returned by a federal grand jury in the District of Columbia, Stevens was convicted of seven counts of making false statements related to his financial disclosure forms. (http://www.usdoj.gov/opa/pr/2008/July/08-crm-668.html). In March, 2009, the conviction was overturned, because of prosecutorial misconduct. Several of the prosecutors now face criminal charges.

Tom Daschle (D, SD), was a senator from January 6, 1987 – January 3, 2005 and United States Senate Majority Leader from June 6, 2001 – January 3, 2003. After he left the Senate, he overlooked taxes on income earned for consulting work and the use of a car service. He also falsified his charitable contributions.

Speaker of the U. S. House of Representatives Jim Wright (D, TX) became the target of an inquiry by the House Ethics Committee. According to Wikipedia (http://en.wikipedia.org/wiki/Jim_Wright): "Their report in early 1989 implied that he had used bulk purchases of his vanity book, Reflections of a Public Man, to earn speaking fees in excess of the allowed maximum, and that his wife, Betty, was given a job and perks to avoid the limit on gifts. Faced with an increasing loss of effectiveness, he resigned as Speaker on May 31, 1989, effective upon the selection of a successor. On June 6, the Democratic caucus brought his Speakership to an end by selecting his replacement, Tom Foley, and on June 30 he resigned from his seat in Congress."

Majority Leader of the House of Representatives Tom DeLay (R, TX) had to leave Congress because of criminal activity. Tom Delay was indicted in 2005 on criminal charges of conspiracy to violate election laws in 2002 by a Travis County, Texas grand jury. He was pressured by his colleagues in Congress not to run for reelection in 2006.

Dan Rostenkowski (D, IL) served in the House of Representatives from 1959 to 1995. He became Chairman of the House Ways and Means Committee in 1981. According to Wikipedia (http://en.wikipedia.org/wiki/Dan_Rostenkowski): "Rostenkowski's political career was shattered in 1994, when he was indicted on corruption charges for his key role in the House post office scandal. He was forced to step down from all Congressional leadership positions. In elections later that year, Rostenkowski lost his seat and retired from political life. Charges against Rostenkowski included keeping "ghost" employees on his payroll, using Congressional funds to buy gifts such as chairs and ashtrays for friends, and trading in officially purchased stamps for cash at the House post office. In 1996, he pleaded guilty to reduced charges of mail fraud. He was fined and was sentenced to 17 months in prison, of which he served 15. Rostenkowski was pardoned in Dec. 2000 by US President Bill Clinton."

Rep. Randy "Duke" Cunningham (D, CA) of the 50th Congressional District of California resigned from Congress in 1995 after pleading guilty to taking more than $2 million in bribes in a criminal conspiracy involving at least three defense contractors.

Former Congressman Robert W. Ney (R, OH) was sentenced to 30 months in prison to be followed by two years of supervised release and fined $6,000. During his supervised release he must serve 100 hours of public service each year. Ney pleaded guilty on October 13, 2006, to a two-count information charging him with conspiracy to commit multiple offenses – including honest services fraud, making false statements, and violations of his former chief of staff's one-year lobbying ban – and with making false statements to the U. S. House of Representatives.

Congressman William Jefferson (D, LA) is serving his 9th term, having represented the 2nd District of Louisiana since 1991. He has been indicted on a host of federal corruption charges, including bribery and violation of the Foreign Corrupt Practices Act. Documents released by the Department of Justice claim that the veteran Democratic lawmaker involved multiple family members in his alleged criminal scheme, which was said to include proposed bribes to a Nigerian official in return for a potentially lucrative telecom contract for a firm secretly controlled by the congressman. Despite a video of Jefferson reportedly accepting $100,000 in payments from an FBI informant, and an FBI raid on his house which yielded $90,000 hidden in the freezer, Jefferson was reelected to Congress in 2006. On August 5, 2009, he was found guilty on 11 of 16 counts, including bribery, racketeering, and money laundering. (See USA Today, August 6, 2009, p. 4A for details).

Congressman Mark Foley (R, FL), Chair of the House Ethics Committee, sent lewd e-mail messages to underage House male pages, creating a national scandal. He was forced to resign his seat in Congress. His successor as Chair of the House Ethics Committee, Tim Mahoney (D, FL), was having a sexual affair with one of his employees. When he broke off the affair, she threatened to sue him and received a $121,000 settlement (New York Times, October 14, 2008, p. A12).

Congressman Charles Rangel (D, NY), Chair of the House Ways and Means Committee, which writes the federal tax code, "forgot" to report $70,000 of income on his tax return, as reported in the New York Times of September 5, 2008.

Lobbyist Jack Abramoff conducted illegal activities with several Congressmen. All of their names have not been revealed at the time of publication of this book.

At the end of 2008, a bipartisan report of the Senate Armed Services Committee made a strong case for bringing criminal charges against former Defense Secretary Donald Rumsfeld; his legal counsel, William J. Haynes; and potentially other top officials, including the former White House Counsel Alberto Gonzales (who later became U. S. Attorney General); and David Addington, Vice President Richard Cheney's former chief of staff. When the issue of torture was brought to the military, all the services and their legal staffs objected. Torture was not instituted as U. S. Policy until Defense Secretary Rumsfeld ordered the military to do so.

Governor Elliot Spitzer (D, NY), a zealous crime fighter when he was attorney general of NY, had to resign from office, when it was learned that he was transporting prostitutes across state lines for indecent purposes (a federal crime).

George Ryan (R, IL), a former governor of Illinois was sentenced to prison for accepting improper campaign contributions. Governor Rod Blagojevich (D, IL) of Illinois and his Chief of Staff, John Harris, were arrested by federal marshals on December, 9, 2008. They were charged with several corruption crimes. One of the more spectacular was the attempt to sell the appointment of the U. S. Senate seat to replace Senator Barack Obama, who had just been elected U. S. President. See TIME magazine of December 22, 2008, pp. 28–30 and the New York Times of December 10, 2008, pp. A1 and A31 for more details.

Ernie Preate (R, PA), a former attorney general of Pennsylvania, was sent to prison for mail fraud while in office. After serving his time in prison, he realized that prison looked a lot different from inside than from the attorney general's office. Since his release, he has dedicated himself to prison reform.

According to the New York Times of Sunday, December 14, 2008, in "The News of the Week in Review," page 3, the U. S. Department of Justice reported that for the decade from 1998–2007, there were 9263 convictions in federal public corruption cases in DC, the 50 states, and the three territories. Undoubtedly there were many more criminal federal, state, and local officials who have not been identified.

C. GOVERNMENT THEFT

On December 17, 2008, Felipe Sixto, who resigned on March 28, 2008, from his job as special assistant to President George Bush for intergovernmental affairs, pleaded guilty to stealing $579,274 from The Center for a Free Cuba, a government funded center. The Center for a Free Cuba describes itself as an independent, nonpartisan institution dedicated to promoting human rights and a transition to democracy and the rule of law in Cuba. It receives millions of dollars a year from USAID. Sixto worked for the center from 2005 to 2007. He joined the Bush administration's Office of Intergovernmental Affairs in July 2007 and was assigned to deal with state legislators, Native American groups and Hispanic officials on issues such as Cuba, Puerto Rico, health, labor, transportation, the environment and energy. (http://www.usatoday.com/news/washington/2008-12-19-bush-aide-cuba_N.htm?csp=34).

Bernard Kerick, Police Commissioner of New York City from 2000–2001 during the Guliani "law and order" administration, committed several crimes. In 2006, Kerik pled guilty to two unrelated ethics violations after an investigation by the Bronx District Attorney's Office, and was ordered to pay $221,000. A grand jury issued a multi-count indictment on November 8, 2007, alleging conspiracy, mail fraud, wire fraud and lying to the Internal Revenue Service. On November 5, 2009, he pleaded guilty to eight charges including tax fraud, false statements on loan applications, and lying to White House officials (New York Times, CLIX NO.54,851, p. A1 (November 6, 2009). As part of a plea bargain, charges of corruption charges and "business activities abroad" were dropped.

The police run the largest criminal operation in the United States, in fact, comparable to all others combined. A U. S. Justice Department report stated that Federal Government seizures alone in fiscal 2006 were $1.718 billion. The U. S. Government Accounting Office in 1998 reported massive waste and loss with the seized loot. The waste and loss within the system are euphemistic terms for looting by federal agents, who then sell the items (primarily drugs).

In 2007, over 9.8 million property crimes were reported to police totaling $17.6 billion (http://www.fbi.gov/ucr/cius2007/). Asset forfeiture without charging the owner of the assets with a crime is the preferred method of theft by law enforcement officials. If the owner is charged with a crime, he or she gets a trial. At the trial, the prosecutor must find the owner guilty beyond reasonable doubt of criminal behavior. Otherwise the assets are returned to the owner. However if the owner is not charged with a crime, the burden of proof is shifted from the state to the owner. The law enforcement officials can keep the property unless the owner can prove beyond a reasonable doubt that the property was never used for a criminal purpose. This is almost impossible to do. According to the Pittsburgh Press, 80% of seizure victims are never even charged with a crime. Some confiscated property is not even recorded by police departments.

Several incidents of asset forfeiture have been described by Jarret B. Wollstein on the web page http://www.isil.org/resources/lit/looting-of- america.html. According to Wollstein: " To get a trial, you have to post a nonrefundable "bond" of 10% of the value of your property. You have to pay attorney fees – ranging from $5,000 to over $100,000 – out of your own pocket. Money you pay your attorney is also subject to seizure (either before or after the trial) if the government alleges that those funds were "tainted." And you may be forced to go through trial after trial, because under civil seizure the Constitutional protection against "double jeopardy" doesn't apply. Once your property is seized, expect to spend years fighting government agencies and expect to be impoverished by legal fees – with no guarantee of winning – while the government keeps your car, home and bank account."

D. POLICE BRUTALITY

The police also beat and kill people with impunity. There have been reported killings, beatings, framings, and drug dealings by the police of Los Angeles in the 1990s (http://www.rense.com/general5/policeds.htm).

Human Rights Watch published reports of police brutality through the 1990s in 14 major U. S. cities (http://www.hrw.org/reports98/police/toc.htm). One case reported there was the torture of Abner Louima. A synopsis of the story reported there follows:

> "In the early morning hours of August 9, 1997, police officers arrested Abner Louima, a legal Haitian immigrant, outside a Brooklyn nightclub following altercations between police and club goers. During the trip to the station house, officers allegedly stopped twice to beat Louima, who was handcuffed. At the 70th Precinct station house, two officers, Justin Volpe and Charles Schwarz, allegedly shouted racial slurs and Volpe allegedly shoved a wooden stick (believed to be the handle of a toilet plunger or broom) into Louima's rectum and mouth. Volpe reportedly borrowed gloves from another officer and walked through the station house with the wooden stick, which was covered with blood and excrement; the gloves were recovered, but the wooden stick was not found on the scene."

"When Louima was taken to a hospital, doctors confirmed that his internal injuries were consistent with his story. Internal organs were ruptured, and his front teeth were broken. For further details, see http://www.thesmokinggun.com/torture/torture.html.

Another incident, reported by WNBC on September 19, 2002, and updated on October 4, 2008, happened in the very same precinct where Abner Louima was brutally attacked. In fact, the officer involved was assigned there right after the Louima torture case to diversify the station house. Now, that officer is charged with a vicious assault that was all captured on home video. In the video, one can see 26-year-old Anthony Carty, already in handcuffs, being subdued by at least six police officers.

Prison Planet reported that in Gwinnett County, GA 31-year old Frederick Williams was struck with a TASER five times in 43 seconds just 4 minutes after being led into the jail, resulting in his death on May 25, 2004. No charges were filed by the county district attorney, who failed to show a video of the incident to a Grand Jury, even though another man in custody was murdered just months earlier after being tortured with a TASER by the same police. More information on this and other incidents, is at: (http://www.prisonplanet.com/articles/september2007/210907_b_brutality.htm).

Rodney King, a black man, was beaten continually in 1991 by several Los Angeles police officers while he was lying on the ground. George Holliday, a bystander, took a video of the beating, which can be seen at: www.youtube.com/watch?v=ROn_9302UHg. The video shows four LA police officers restraining and repeatedly striking a black man, while four to six other officers stand by. King had also been tasered by the officers. The police were charged with using excessive force. A Los

Angeles judge decided that an impartial jury could not be found in Los Angeles County, a county with a diverse population of over 4 million people. So the case was moved to San Bernardino County, where many police officers lived, and the population was hostile to black people. The jury found the police officers not guilty. The announcement of the acquittals sparked the 1992 Los Angeles riots.

The police murder of Amadou Diallo on February 4, 1999 is described in some detail on pp. 189–197 in the book "Blink" by Malcolm Gladwell (Little, Brown, and Company, New York, 1995). Mr. Diallo, a 22-year old immigrant from Guinea, was standing in front of the apartment in which he lived when he was spotted by four white policemen in plain clothes driving an unmarked Ford Taurus. They thought he might be involved in some criminal activity, though he was not. He was just enjoying the fresh air.

The police approached him, so Mr. Diallo went into the building to return to his apartment. The police followed him. As he reached his apartment, he reached into his pocket and withdrew his wallet. The police thought that he had drawn a gun, so they pumped 41 bullets into him and killed him. Bruce Springsteen wrote a song in Mr. Diallo's honor called "41 shots," with the chorus "You can get killed just for living in your American skin."

Sean Bell was killed by police on his wedding day. His bride-to-be received his corpse as a wedding present. The incident is described by Wikipedia (http://en.wikipedia.org/wiki/Sean_Bell) as follows:

> "The Sean Bell shooting incident took place in the New York City borough of Queens on November 25, 2006, in which one Latino and two African-American men were shot at a total of fifty times by a team of both plainclothes and undercover NYPD

> officers (two of whom were themselves African-American), killing one of the men, Sean Bell, on the morning of his wedding day, and severely wounding two of his friends.[1] The incident sparked fierce criticism of the police from some members of the public and drew comparisons to the 1999 killing of Amadou Diallo.[2] Three of the five detectives involved in the shooting went to trial [3] on charges ranging from manslaughter to reckless endangerment, and were found not guilty."[4] (see the web page for references).

On November 23, 2008, the New York Post reported that a team of NYPD narcotics cops is under investigation for arresting four men in a Queens club after surveillance tapes revealed the cops never bought drugs from them. The stunning accusations stem from a "buy-and-bust" operation in January when undercover cops allegedly framed two brothers and their friends who were merely drinking beer and chatting inside Club Delicioso in Elmhurst. The quartet was originally charged with selling two bags of cocaine worth $100 (http://www.nypost.com/seven/06282008/news/regionalnews/cop_team_probed_in__drug_frame_shame_117572.htm).

On December 10, 2008, the New York Times, page A1 reported that Richard Kern, a New York City patrolman, used his baton to sodomize Michael Mineo in a subway station, and two complicit colleagues helped him cover it up. Mr. Mineo suffered a crushed anus and blood on his hands.

Bob Herbert, in the New York Times of August 4, 2009, p. A23, reports that the police in Avon Park, FL, armcuff and arrest 6-year old children for throwing tantrums. The sheriff admits to this.

Other infamous police misdeeds occurred earlier in the second half of the 20th century. In his capacity as Commissioner of

Public Safety for Birmingham, Alabama, Eugene "Bull" Connor ordered police dogs and water hoses to be used to control freedom marchers in Selma, Alabama in May, 1963.

Andrew Goodman, James Chaney, and Michael Schwermer were three American civil rights activists who were murdered near Philadelphia, Mississippi, during Freedom Summer in 1964 by members of the Ku Klux Klan on June 21, 1964. The Sheriff of Neshoba County was implicated in the murders.

There was a police riot in Chicago seen on national television during the Democratic party nominating convention in 1968. A video of the riot can be seen at http://www.youtube.com/watch?v=6FDuCfRaj5w.

Four unarmed students at Kent State University in Cleveland, OH (Allison Krause, Jeffrey Miller, Sandra Scheuer and William Knox Schroeder) were killed on May 4, 1970 while protesting the invasion of Cambodia by the United States, when the Ohio National Guard opened fire on them, firing at least 67 shots.

The shootings led to protests and a national student strike, causing hundreds of campuses to close because of both violent and nonviolent demonstrations. The Kent State campus remained closed for six weeks. Five days after the shootings, 100,000 people demonstrated in Washington, D. C. against the war.

In addition to the above violent crimes, police harassment occurs daily in major U. S. cities. The homeless, women whom the police think may be engaged in prostitution, and demonstrators (particularly for unpopular causes) routinely are harassed.

In the New York Times of May 26, 2007, on page A13, columnist Bob Herbert states that young men and women, particularly blacks and Hispanics, are routinely stopped, searched, harassed, intimidated, and sometimes, arrested for no good reason at all. He describes an incident in Brooklyn where about three dozen grieving young people on their way to a wake for a murdered teenage friend were surrounded by the police, cursed, handcuffed, and ordered into paddy wagons. Several were thrown into jail. There was no indication that the teenagers were misbehaving in any way. Some were carrying notes from school allowing them to be absent to attend the wake. In his column in the New York Times of April 18, 2009, Bob Herbert reported that all the charges were dismissed, some even by the prosecuting attorneys. The youngsters sued the police, and 16 of them were each given between $9000 and $23,000 in a settlement.

On March 13, 2010, in the New York Times. p. A19, Bob Herbert pointed out that the NY City police keep a data base of all New Yorkers who are stopped, questioned, and often frisked by police. More than 575,000 stops were made in 2009, but in 504,594 of those stops, the individuals had done nothing wrong. Yet they were kept in the data base.

The New York City police are even killing themselves. On May 31, 2009, the New York Times front page reported that police officer Omar J. Edwards was fatally shot by police officer Andrew P. Dutton shortly after 10:30 pm on May 28, 2009. Both had guns in their hands. Neither was in uniform. Edwards was mistakenly suspected as being a thief by three other officers in an unmarked car. They shot and killed him. The problem here is that plain clothes police officers were brandishing guns. If they are doing detective work, they should call on officers in police uniform to enforce the law.

In 2006, police officer Eric Hernandez was shot dead in the Bronx by a fellow officer outside a White Castle.

II. THE JEW HATERS

A. IRAN

Mahmoud Ahmadinejad, the 6th President of Iran, is the modern day reincarnation of Adolph Hitler. He believes the Muslims are the master race and that the state of Israel should be obliterated and the Jews removed therefrom. He addressed the UN General Assembly several times. In his UN speeches he advocates the destruction of Israel.

Ahmadinejad told students at a conference in Tehran called The World Without Zionism: "Anyone who recognizes Israel will burn in the fire of the Islamic nation's fury. Any Islamic leader who recognizes the Zionist regime means he acknowledges the surrender and defeat of the Islamic world."

Iran is the primary financial supporter and trains the terrorists of Hizbullah, Hamas, and Islamic Jihad.

B. HIZBULLAH

Hizbullah, the 'Party of God' was founded in the early 1980s with the backing of the Iranian Revolutionary Guards. This Shiite Islamic fundamentalist organization is an armed political party with members in the Lebanese parliament. Its repeated clashes with Israel culminated in the 2006 summer war in Lebanon and it is currently engaged in an intense power-struggle over Lebanon's political future

Hizbullah leaders have also made numerous statements calling for the destruction of Israel, which they refer to as a "Zionist entity... built on lands wrested from their owners."

C. HAMAS

Hamas is the democratically elected government of the Palestinian Authority. The principles of Hamas are stated in their

Covenant or Charter (http://www.mideastweb.org/hamas.htm). Following are highlights:

From the Preamble of the Hamas Charter: "Israel will exist and will continue to exist until Islam will obliterate it, just as it obliterated others before it"

From Article 7 of the Hamas Charter:

"The Day of Judgment will not come about until Muslims fight Jews and kill them. Then, the Jews will hide behind rocks and trees, and the rocks and trees will cry out: 'O Muslim, there is a Jew hiding behind me, come and kill him,'"

From Article 11 of the Hamas Charter:

"The Islamic Resistance Movement believes that the land of Palestine is an Islamic Waqf consecrated for future Moslem generations until Judgement Day. It, or any part of it, should not be squandered: it, or any part of it, should not be given up."

From Article 13 of the Hamas Charter:

"There is no solution for the Palestinian problem except by jihad. Initiatives, proposals and international conferences are but a waste of time, an exercise in futility."

From Hamas official web site video, February 2006:

"My message to the loathed Jews...We are a nation that drinks blood, and we know that there is no blood better than the blood of Jews. We will not leave you alone until we have quenched our thirst with your blood. We will not leave until you leave the Muslim countries."

The socio-political makeup of "Hamastan" (a Palestinian radical Islamist state, ruled by Hamas), as described in interviews granted by Mahmoud al-Zahar, a senior Hamas figure in the Gaza Strip: "The continuation of the violent confrontation against Israel until its annihilation." Mahmoud al-Zahar attributes to the Zionist movement the desire to take over the region between the Euphrates and the Nile and expresses a radical world view seeking to establish an Islamic Palestinian state across the entire territory of Palestine, including the territory of the State of Israel.

Mahmoud al-Zahar's statements were made following Israel's disengagement from the Gaza Strip and prior to the Legislative Council elections, a transition period characterized by significant tension between the Palestinian Authority and Hamas.

In summary, Hamas' world view with regard to the makeup of the Palestinian state, as it is reflected in Al-Zahar's interviews, is as follows: A Palestinian state of radical Islamic character, an extension of the radical Islamic stream led by the Muslim Brotherhood, which holds close contacts with Islamic Arab countries. It is a state where secular and non-Islamic (Christian) elements will be forced to embrace radical Islamist codes in all walks of life; it is a state that does not cooperate and severs its ties with Israel and Western countries, holds close contacts with other Islamic Arab countries (obviously, with radical Islamic movements as well), and embraces a strategy of armed struggle (i.e., terrorism) against Israel until its annihilation. Such a state would be, in fact, of a radical Islamic nature. It will be run by Hamas, the state of "Hamastan". Indeed, when asked by a Newsweek reporter (August 30, 2005) whether the Gaza Strip would become "Hamastan", Mahmoud al-Zahar responded: "It should be Hamastan."

D. ISLAMIC RESISTANCE MOVEMENT

The Covenant of the Islamic Resistance Movement, 18 August 1988, from Article 7 In The Name Of The Most Merciful Allah:

"The Day of Judgement will not come about until Moslems fight the Jews (killing the Jews), when the Jew will hide behind stones and trees. The stones and trees will say O Moslems, O Abdulla, there is a Jew behind me, come and kill him. Only the Gharkad tree, (evidently a certain kind of tree) would not do that because it is one of the trees of the Jews." (related by al-Bukhari and Moslem).

From Wikipedia, the free encyclopedia :
(http://en.wikipedia.org/wiki/Palestinian_Islamic_Jihad)

"The emblem of the Palestinian Islamic Jihad (PIJ) shows a map of the land they claim as Palestine (roughly, present-day Israel, the West Bank and the Gaza Strip) superimposed on the images of the Dome of the Rock, two fists and two rifles."

"Palestinian Islamic Jihad is a militant group, regarded as terrorist by Israel, the United States and the European Union, whose goal is the 'liberation' of historical Palestine, destruction of the State of Israel and its replacement with an Islamist state for Palestinians."

"This group defines jihad as acts of war against Israelis. Palestinian Islamic Jihad also opposes many other Arab governments, who they see as being insufficiently Islamic and too western. The PIJ's armed wing , the Al- Quds brigades, has claimed responsibility for numerous militant attacks in Israel, including suicide bombings."

"Unlike the far larger Hamas, which split from it, the Islamic Jihad has a smaller support base, and no real social or political role. The Palestinian Islamic Jihad was formed in the Gaza Strip during the 1970s by Fathi Shaqaqi as a branch of the Egyptian Islamic Jihad."

"Shaqaqi led the organization for two decades. He was killed in Malta in October 1995 by an unknown party. Some people believe the party to be Israel, while others say other Palestinian groups killed him. The Palestinian Islamic Jihad often attempts to carry out attacks against Israeli targets on the anniversary of his death, although the identity of the assassins was never determined."

"The group is based in the Syrian capital, Damascus, and its financial backing is believed to come from there and Iran. The group operates primarily in the West Bank and Gaza Strip, but has also carried out attacks in Jordan and Lebanon. Its main strongholds in the West Bank are the cities of Hebron and Jenin."

"During the Al-Aqsa Intifada the PIJ committed many suicide bombing attacks against Israelis. Many of the attacks in 2001 and 2002 came from the PIJ in Jenin, headed by Mahmoud Tawallbe, Ali Sefoori and Tabeth Mardawi. The headquarters of the PIJ in Jenin and the West Bank was seriously damaged during Operation Defensive Shield: Tawalle was killed by an IDF Caterpillar D9 armored bulldozer while Sefoori and Mardawi were arrest by Israel security forces."

"On February 20, 2003, University of South Florida computer engineering professor Dr. Sami Al-Arian was arrested after being indicted on 50 "terrorism' related charges. US Attorney General John Ashcroft alleged at a press conference that Dr. Al-Arian is the North American head of the Palestinian Islamic Jihad."

"Islamic Jihad is alleged to have used women and teens as suicide bombers. On March 29, 2004, 16-year-old Tamer Khuweir in Rifidia, an Arab suburb of Shechem was apprehended by Israeli security forces as he prepared to carry out a suicide attack. His older brother claimed he was brainwashed to do it by an Islamic Jihad cleric, and demanded the Palestinian Authority to investigate the incident and arrest those responsible to it." [1]

E. FATAH

Fatah is another of the Jew-hating groups. It is the descendant of the Palestine Liberation Organization, (PLO) founded and controlled by Yasar Arafat until his death.

The Fatah official emblem shows two fists holding rifles and a hand grenade superimposed on a map of the land they claim as Palestine (roughly, present-day Israel, the West Bank and the Gaza Strip). (http://en.wikipedia.org/wiki/Fatah)

III. INCIDENT OF APRIL 17, 2007

A. THE DEMONSTRATION

On April 17, 2007, President Mahmoud Ahmadinejad of Iran addressed the UN General assembly in New York City. Rabbi Avi Weiss of the Hebrew Institute of Riverdale in the Bronx organized a demonstration against Mahmoud Ahmadinejad and Iran. About 25 rabbis dressed in religious garb, along with about 50–100 other demonstrators, including me, gathered in front of the Iranian embassy in Manhattan at noon on that day and held a rally. Several rabbis gave short speeches denouncing President Mahmoud Ahmadinejad and Iran.

Then the group marched to the Isaiah Wall across the street from the UN Building where President Mahmoud Ahmadinejad would give his speech. During the march, the group displayed banners, blew on ram's horns (shofars), and sang songs of support for Israel. At the Isaiah Wall, the rabbis again gave short speeches and then sat down on the steps in front of the Isaiah Wall, blocking pedestrian traffic. The other demonstrators were carrying signs, blowing rams' horns, and using electronic audio equipment. The police did not object to any of the activities of the other demonstrators.

The police warned the rabbis several times that unless they moved, they would be arrested. The rabbis refused to move.

The police asked the other demonstrators to move back, so as not to interfere with the arrests. This was a reasonable request, and the demonstrators proceeded to move back. However, the police kept moving the demonstrators further and further back until they were 35 feet behind the nearest rabbi.

The Isaiah wall is curved, so that the demonstrators were moved so far back that they could no longer be seen from the street. It was apparent that the intent of the police was to disband the demonstration. I alone moved forward to 13 feet behind the rabbis and was visible from the street.

I stood next to the guard rail, which was 8 feet from the Isaiah wall, holding two signs, both of which read: "**STOP HATING JEWS**." I was silent and made no hand or foot gestures. There was no interference with pedestrian traffic. The police did not object or say anything to me while they were arresting the rabbis. However after all the rabbis were arrested and removed, I was approached by the police and asked to move back with the other demonstrators.

The Demonstration just before the arrests.
Rabbi Avi Weiss, who organized the demonstration, is sitting front center of the rabbis. The author is on the left in the rear holding the signs that say **STOP HATING JEWS**.

B. THE ARREST

After all of the rabbis were arrested, there was no one in front of me for at least 40 feet or behind me for at least 22 feet. I was standing alone next to the chain railing 8 feet from the Isaiah wall. The police approached me and asked me to move back with the other demonstrators, 22 feet behind me. I refused saying that I was not bothering anyone. The police repeated that I must move back to the other demonstrators or be arrested. I insisted that I had the right to be there, and that an arrest could result in a law suit.

The police then put me under arrest and reached for me. I went limp. The police did not catch me, and I fell to the ground, lay still, and made no sound.

A woman approached me, introduced herself as a nurse, and asked if I was all right. I did not answer at first. She pleaded with the police that I was an old man, and that they should not arrest me. After some pleading, the police agreed on the condition that I would leave the location and join the other demonstrators. I sat up, assured the woman that I was OK, and stood up.

I told the police that I would not leave, that I had a permit to be there. I read to the police officers the First Amendment from a pocket U. S. Constitution.

The police said that I would be arrested. I asked for what reason, and was told for refusing to obey the order of a law enforcement officer. No mention was made of disorderly conduct or any of the specific items of disorderly conduct (NY Penal Code §240.20).

I went limp and fell to the ground. From then until in a jail cell at police headquarters for some time, I did not move a muscle or utter any sound.

When on the ground, the police lifted and dragged me to the police wagon, carried me into the wagon, and placed me into a holding cell at police headquarters. I did not move a muscle nor utter any sound until approached by medics from the fire department.

As far as I could tell, no-one except the police officers were anywhere in my vicinity at the time of the confrontation and arrest. I was unaware that anyone else was arrested together with me.

An improper arrest often is called euphemistically a false arrest by law enforcement personnel. False means it did not occur. This was no false arrest. It was real. I spent 22 hours in confinement.

On April 19, 2007, I went to Property Control at Police Headquarters Security to reclaim my property. Sergeant Rufulo and Police officer Privleau returned my cell phone, but claimed that they did not have my demonstration signs or any record of them.

This arrest might be called an illegal arrest. To me, an illegal arrest would mean that the police officers thought that they were acting legally, but were mistaken. No such doubt existed here, since I read to the officers the First Amendment to the U. S. Constitution. The officers knew that they were breaking the law, but did not care.

Thus this act of confinement was a kidnapping, plain and simple. It was accompanied by theft, since my signs were confiscated and not returned. Furthermore the police were involved in reckless endangerment when they ordered me to move into a crowd with signs, rams' horns, and electronic equipment. Also the police were ordering me to participate in a crime, since the other demonstrators were blocking pedestrian traffic.

C. POLICE ALLEGATIONS

In the arrest report, the police allege that:

> "...the defendant intentionally attempted to prevent a police officer and peace officer from effecting an authorized arrest of himself and another person; the

> defendant intentionally prevented and attempted to prevent a public servant from performing an official function by intimidation, physical force and interference and by means of an independently unlawful act; the defendant, with intent to cause public inconvenience, annoyance and alarm and recklessly creating a risk thereof, obstructing vehicular and pedestrian traffic; and the defendant, with intent to cause public inconvenience, annoyance and alarm and recklessly creating a risk thereof, congregated in a public place with other persons and refused to comply with a lawful order of the police to disperse."

I admit to refusing to comply with an order of the police, because it was unlawful. The other allegations were never made at the time of arrest, even though I asked for the reasons for arrest. They were manufactured later. All of them are untrue.

At the bottom of the form signed by Deponent Jason Toala, there is a statement that reads: "False statements made herein are punishable as a class A misdemeanor pursuant to section 210.45 of the penal law." Thus Deponent Toala will be guilty of perjury, if he repeats these statements under oath, along with the other crimes of kidnapping and theft.

Let us consider these allegations individually:

I never attempted to prevent an authorized arrest of myself and another person. There was no other person placed under arrest or even in the vicinity at the time of arrest. I was standing still and holding two signs when I was placed under arrest. After I was placed under arrest I went limp and fell to the ground, because the police officers failed to catch me.

There was no intimidation, physical force and interference after the arrest, because I was lying on the ground completely silent and motionless. I was carried and dragged to the patrol wagon. I did not resist handcuffing, which was readily effected.

I did not cause public inconvenience, annoyance and alarm. At the time of the arrest, I was standing still and alone displaying two signs, but uttering no sounds or making any facial, arm, or leg motions. In any case, actions after the arrest is made cannot be a cause for arrest.

I was next to the guard rail, 8 feet from the wall, 22 feet in front of the other demonstrators, and at least 40 feet from the street. I could not have been obstructing either vehicular or pedestrian traffic. Pedestrians were passing by me routinely near the wall 8 feet away.

I was not congregating with other people. In fact that was the bone of contention. The police ordered me to congregate with the others, but I refused because the order was a violation of my constitutional right to peaceful protest, would have recklessly endangered me, and would have made me a participant in a crime (blocking pedestrian traffic).

I was not ordered to disperse. In fact it would have been impossible to do so, since I was standing alone. I was ordered to congregate.

D. ARRAIGNMENT

The arraignment occurred on April 18, 2007, in the Criminal Court of the City of New York, County of New York (commonly known as the Criminal Court of Manhattan).

Neither the arraignment magistrate nor the prosecuting assistant district attorney were identified to me or to any of the other arrestees, in keeping with the procedures of a court of inquisition.

About 15 other arrestees were arraigned before me. All of them, except for one man, pleaded guilty.

The exceptional arrestee pleaded not guilty several times, even though the Court would not accept this plea and kept asking him to reconsider. Finally one of the court stenographers yelled: "Plead guilty. You know that you are guilty." At this point the arrestee's court-appointed counsel pleaded guilty for the arrestee. So much for the presumption of innocence.

Another arrestee was a 19-year old black woman. She was eating dinner at a restaurant when she was arrested and strip searched. Cocaine was found in her brassiere. It did not occur to anyone to inquire if the police had a search warrant. Apparently the quaint custom of search warrants is discarded ancient English law.

When my turn occurred, the magistrate first asked if I had attended school and, if so, what was my highest degree. I, who at the time was 75 years old, responded that I had not attended school recently, but that my highest degree was a Ph. D. in chemistry, and that I was a professor of chemistry. I still do not understand why this information was any of the magistrate's business.

I then was asked if I had legal counsel. I replied that I would be acting as counsel *pro se*. I said that I had tried about 40 cases, but none in New York state. I said that I was unaware of New York laws or court procedures and that I could use an advisory counsel.

At that point the Court appointed Edward McCarthy, Supervising Attorney, Criminal Defense Division, The Legal Aid Society, 100 Centre Street, Room 511, New York, NY 10013 (Telephone: 212–571–5930) as temporary advisory counsel. Coincidentally, the Court had already positioned Mr. McCarthy at my side in the dock.

I then was advised by the magistrate that before I pleaded, the prosecuting assistant district attorney had a plea bargain. The prosecuting assistant district attorney offered to settle for time served (22 hours), if I would plead guilty. I replied: "If I was willing to accept that, I would not have bothered to be arrested in the first place."

The magistrate asked: "Are you pleading not guilty?" She then warned (threatened) me that, if so, I could go to prison. I acknowledged that I was aware that a prison sentence was possible. I then pleaded not guilty, demanded indictment by a Grand Jury, and asked for a jury trial.

After the stunned Court recovered, the magistrate did not object to the plea or the demand for indictment by a Grand Jury. She had no idea of what the charges were, since she had to ask the prosecuting assistant district attorney if I was entitled to a jury trial. The answer was affirmative.

I was told that I must report for a court hearing on June 20, 2007, and submit all informations before May 17, 2007. I asked the purpose of the hearing, but my question was ignored. No written **ORDER** was issued to appear for the hearing date of June 20, 2007.

I was handed the unsigned arraignment form with the police charges and released after 22 hours of confinement. I was not committed at arraignment nor at any other time. I have not been indicted nor informed that any Grand Jury has been convened.

A few days later, I was contacted by Simone Levine, an attorney at The Legal Aid Society, and informed that the prosecuting assistant district attorney was willing to drop the charges and dismiss the case, if I would agree to not get arrested in the next 6 months and not sue the police. I declined.

It is not clear to me why the prosecuting assistant District Attorney did not contact me directly. It seems to me that it is improper for the District Attorney's office to be conducting negotiations with anyone but the Defendant or his counsel.

The function of the district attorney is to prosecute crime, not to protect it. He should be prosecuting the police, not protecting them. By protecting them, the prosecuting assistant district attorney is an accessory to the crimes of kidnapping and theft. He should be dismissed from his position and disbarred.

IV. INDICTMENT BY GRAND JURY

The Fifth Amendment to the U. S. Constitution requires indictment by a Grand Jury to try capital or other infamous crimes. Unfortunately, neither the U. S. Constitution nor the Congress nor the Courts ever defined infamous crimes. The custom in U. S. federal courts is to treat infamous crimes as those which carry a maximum sentence of over 1 year in prison. New York State follows the same practice. These crimes are called felonies. Crimes with lesser sentences are called misdemeanors.

However other states follow other practices. In New Jersey, a felony is a crime with a maximum sentence exceeding 6 months in prison and requires a Grand Jury indictment. In Pennsylvania, the legislature abolished Grand Jury indictments for all crimes, even capital crimes [PA. CONST. art. I, § 10 and 42 Pa.C.S. § 8931 (b)]. There are no Grand Jury indictments in Pennsylvania courts. In Pennsylvania, the Bill of Rights is void when prohibited by state law.

Needless to say, these various interpretations violate Amendment XIV, Section 1 of the U. S. Constitution, which guarantees equal protection under the law. Therefore I wrote a brief on July 2, 2007, to the Criminal Court of Manhattan discussing the requirements for Grand Jury indictment. The Court never responded to my Brief (or any other document that I submitted).

Because there is general confusion in the legal profession regarding the necessity of Grand Jury indictment, that Brief follows:

CRIMINAL COURT OF THE CITY OF NEW YORK
COUNTY OF NEW YORK

The People of the State of New York
Prosecutor

against — Docket #2007–NY029913

Julian Heicklen
Defendant

BRIEF FOR CONVENING A GRAND JURY

A. CONSTITUTIONAL REQUIREMENTS

1. Article 1, Section 1, §6 of the Constitution of the State of New York states, in part:

> "No person shall be held to answer for a capital or otherwise infamous crime...unless on indictment of a grand jury..."

2. Amendment V of the United States Constitution states, in part:

> "No person shall be held to answer for a capital or otherwise infamous crime...unless on indictment of a grand jury..."

3. Neither of these documents state that a person charged with a lesser crime can be denied indictment by a grand jury.
4. Neither of these documents defines "infamous crime."

B. U. S. SUPREME COURT RULINGS

5. The subject of what constitutes an infamous crime was discussed at length in Ex parte Wilson, 114 U. S. 417 (1885), S.C. 5 Sup. Ct. Rep 935. 38
6. Justice Gray ruled:

> "The leading word 'capital' describing the crime by its punishment only, the associated words 'or otherwise infamous crime' must, by an elementary rule of construction, include crimes subject to any infamous punishment, even if they should [114 U. S. 417, 424] be held to include also crimes infamous in their nature, independently of the punishment affixed to them."
>
> "...this court is of opinion that the competency of the defendant, if convicted, to be a witness in another case is not the true test; and that no person can be held to answer, without presentment or indictment by a grand jury, for any crime for which an infamous punishment may be imposed by the court. The question is whether the crime is one for which the statutes authorize the court to award an infamous punishment not whether the punishment ultimately awarded is an infamous one. When the accused is in danger of being subjected to an infamous punishment if convicted, he has the right to insist that he shall not be put upon his trial, except on the accusation of a grand jury."
>
> "Nor can we accede to the proposition, which has been sometimes maintained, that no crime is infamous, within the meaning of the fifth amendment, that has not been so declared by

congress. See U. S. v. Wynn, 3 McCrary, 266; S. C. 9 Fed. Rep. 886; Same v. Same, 11 Fed. Rep. 57; U. S. v. Petit, 11 Fed. Rep. 58; U. S. v. Cross, 1 McArthur, 149. The purpose of the amendment was to limit the powers of the legislature, as well as of the prosecuting officers, of the United States. We are not, indeed, disposed to deny that a crime, to the conviction and punishment of which congress has superadded a disqualification to hold office, is thereby made infamous. U. S. v. Waddell, 112 U. S. 76 , 82; S. C. ante, 35. But the constitution protecting every one from being prosecuted, without the intervention of a grand jury, for any crime which is subject by law to an infamous punishment, no declaration of congress is needed to secure or competent to defeat the constitutional safeguard."

"The remaining question to be considered is whether imprisonment at hard labor for a term of years is an infamous punishment. Infamous punishments cannot be limited to those punishments which are cruel or unusual, because, by the seventh amendment of the constitution, 'cruel and unusual punishments' are wholly forbidden, and cannot therefore be lawfully [114 U. S. 417, 427] inflicted even in cases of convictions upon indictments duly presented by a grand jury."

"Deciding nothing beyond what is required by the facts of the case before us, our judgment is that a crime punishable by imprisonment for a term of years at hard labor is an infamous crime, within the meaning of the fifth amendment of the constitution; and that the district court, in holding the petitioner to answer for such a crime, and sentencing him to such imprisonment, without indictment or presentment by a grand jury, exceeded its jurisdiction, and he is therefore entitled to be discharged."

7. In Mackin v. U. S., 117 U. S. 348 (1886), Justice Gray ruled:

> "...we cannot doubt that at the present day imprisonment in a state prison or penitentiary, with or without hard labor, is an infamous punishment. It is not only so considered in the general opinion of the people, but it has been recognized in the legislation of the states and territories, as well as of congress."

8. In Mackin v. U. S. (*supra*), there is no mention of the length of time of the imprisonment. According to the Mackin ruling, 1 day in a state prison or penitentiary would be an infamous punishment.
9. Green v. U. S., 356 U. S. 165 (1958) is often quoted as justification for the one-year provision. Defendant has read that opinion carefully and finds no such mention of such a requirement.
10. Even if there were a one-year requirement for Grand Jury indictment, it would not apply to Defendant, who faces charges that could lead to one-year imprisonment plus the one day that he already has served for these charges. This would make his sentence greater than one-year.
11. Whether the crime for which the accused is sentenced is called a felony or a misdemeanor is of no consequence. Only the

maximum length of sentence that can be imposed is relevant.

12. Misdemeanor offenses in New York Penal Law § 70.15 Section 1 provides maximum sentences of 1 year for misdemeanors. However other states have other maximum sentences. For example the maximum sentence in New Jersey is 6 months; in Pennsylvania, it is 2 years.
13. The name of the facility of imprisonment is also of no consequence. A county jail is still a state prison, because it is subject to state oversight. In Pennsylvania some counties have no county jails, only county prisons, to house misdemeanants.
14. Because of overcrowding, misdemeanants are sometimes housed in state facilities in Pennsylvania. Probably also in New York.
15. Because misdemeanants may be housed, even temporarily, in state prisons, Grand Jury requirements must apply to misdemeanor offenses.
16. In Pennsylvania, except for county prisons, there are no state prisons or penitentiaries, only state "correctional institutions." Does this mean that that there are no felonies in Pennsylvania? Or that felons are not incarcerated in state penitentiaries?
17. It is absurd to define infamous crimes by the names given to them or the facilities in which prisoners are housed. There is no such requirement in the court decisions.
18. Neither is there any requirement for the length of incarceration.

C. U. S. ATTORNEY'S MANUAL

19. The U. S. Attorney's Manual §205 states:

> "The courts have ruled that any crime that may be punished by more than one year of imprisonment in a penitentiary or at hard labor is an infamous crime. See Green v. United States, 356 U. S. 165, 183 (1958); Mackin v. United States, 117 U. S. 348, 350–52 (1886)"

20. Defendant could find no such statements in those referenced documents. The reference is even wrong. There were two Green decisions [Green v. United States, 356 U. S. 165 (1958) and Green v. United States, 355 U. S. 183 (1957)].

D. PURPOSE OF THE GRAND JURY

21. In Wood v. Georgia, 370 U. S. 375 (1962), the Supreme Court commented about the purpose of the Grand Jury:

> "Historically, this body has been regarded as a primary security to the innocent against hasty, malicious and oppressive persecution; it serves the invaluable function in our society of standing between the accuser and the accused, whether the latter be an individual, minority group, or other, to determine whether a charge is founded upon reason or was dictated by an intimidating power or by malice and personal ill will. Particularly in matters of local political corruption and investigations is it important that freedom of communication be kept open and that the real issues not become obscured to the grand jury. It cannot effectively operate in a vacuum. It has been said that the "ancestors of our 'grand jurors' are from the first neither exactly accusers, nor exactly witnesses; they are to give

voice to common repute." Pollock and Maitland, History of the English Law (2d ed. 1909), 642. The necessity to society of an independent and informed grand jury becomes readily apparent in the context of the present case. For here a panel of judges, themselves elected officers and charged under state law with the responsibility of instructing a grand jury to investigate political corruption, have exercised the contempt power to hold in contempt another elected representative of the people for publishing views honestly held and contrary to those contained in the charge. And, an [370 U. S. 375, 391] effort by the petitioner to prove the truth of his allegations was rejected, the court holding irrelevant the truth or falsity of the facts and opinions expressed in the publications. 103 Ga. App. 305, 321, 119 S. E. 2d 261, 273. If the petitioner could be silenced in this manner, the problem to the people in the State of Georgia and indeed in all the States becomes evident. The administration of the law is not the problem of the judge or prosecuting attorney alone, but necessitates the active cooperation of an enlightened public. Nothing is to be gained by an attitude on the part of the citizenry of civic irresponsibility and apathy in voicing their sentiments on community problems."

E. CONCLUSION

22. Thus the Grand Jury is not an instrument for the courts to prosecute the citizens. Rather it is an instrument for the citizens to protect themselves against the tyranny of the courts.

Any person charged with a crime that could result in incarceration must be indicted by a Grand Jury.

V. JURY NULLIFICATION

A. Reason for jury trial

The reason to have a jury trial is twofold:

1. In practice the jury will be more impartial than the judge. In a criminal trial, the judge tends to favor conviction, because his standing with the people who pay his salary depends on his ability to get convictions and send people to prison.
2. Furthermore the jury can do something that the judge will not do, *i.e.* nullify the law when justice requires it to do so.

B. History of jury nullification

Juries originally were introduced into England to protect the individual from the tyranny of government. The first case in which juries nullified a law was that of William Penn and William Mead in England in 1670. The jurors refused to convict the two Quaker activists charged with unlawful assembly. The judge refused to accept a verdict other than guilty, and ordered the jurors to resume their deliberations without food or drink. When the jurors persisted in their refusal to convict, the court fined them and committed them to prison until the fines were paid. On appeal, the Court of Common Pleas ordered the jurors released, holding that they could not be punished for their verdict.

Jury nullification was introduced into America in 1735 in the trial of John Peter Zenger, Printer of The New York Weekly Journal. Zenger repeatedly attacked Governor William Cosby of New York in his journal. This was a violation of the seditious libel law, which prohibited criticism of the King or his appointed officers. The attacks became sufficient to bring Zenger to trial. He clearly was guilty of breaking the law, which held that true statements could be libelous. However Zenger's lawyer, Andrew Hamilton, addressed himself to the jury, arguing that the court's law was outmoded. Hamilton contended that falsehood was the principal thing that makes a libel. It took the jury only a few minutes to nullify the law and declare Zenger not guilty. Ever since, the truth has been a defense in libel cases.

Several state constitutions, including the Georgia Constitution of 1777 and the Pennsylvania Constitution of 1790 specifically provided that "the jury shall be judges of law, as well as fact." In Pennsylvania, Supreme Court Justice James Wilson noted, in his Philadelphia law lectures of 1790, that when "a difference in sentiment takes place between the judges and jury, with regard to a point of law,...The jury must do their duty, and their whole duty; They must decide the law as well as the fact." In 1879, the Pennsylvania Supreme Court noted that "the power of the jury to be judge of the law in criminal cases is one of the most valuable securities guaranteed by the Bill of Rights."

John Jay, the first Chief Justice of the U. S. Supreme Court stated in 1789: "The jury has the right to judge both the law as well as the fact in controversy." Samuel Chase, U. S. Supreme Court Justice and signer of the Declaration of Independence, said in 1796: "The jury has the right to determine both the law and the facts. " U. S. Supreme Court Justice Oliver Wendell Holmes said in 1902: "The jury has the power to bring a verdict in the teeth of both law and fact." Harlan F. Stone, the 12th Chief Justice of the U. S. Supreme Court, stated in 1941: "The law itself is on trial quite as much as the cause which is to be decided."

In Morissette v. United States 342 US 246 (1952), the U. S. Supreme Court recognized the powers of juries to engage in nullification. The court stated:

> "Had the jury convicted on proper instructions it would be the end of the matter. But juries are not bound by what seems inescapable logic to judges....They might have refused to brand

Morissette as a thief. Had they done so, that too would have been the end of the matter."

In U. S. v. Dougherty, 473 F 2nd 1113, 1139 (1972), the Court said: "The pages of history shine on instances of the jury's exercise of its prerogative to disregard instructions of the judge."

Likewise, the U. S. Supreme Court in Duncan v. Louisiana, 391 U. S. 145, 156 (1968) implicitly endorsed the policies behind nullification when it stated: "If the defendant preferred the common-sense judgment of the jury to the more tutored but less sympathetic reaction of the single judge, he was to have it."

In recent times, the courts have tried to erode the nullification powers of juries. Particular impetus for this was given by the fact that all-white juries in the southern states refused to convict whites of crimes against blacks. As a result there is a practice of judges to incorrectly instruct the jury that the judge determines the law, and that the jury is limited to determining the facts.

Such an instruction defeats the purpose of the jury, which is to protect the defendant from the tyranny of the state. Judges or expert witnesses can determine the facts better than juries can. The purpose of the jury is to protect the defendant from the tyranny of the law.

The problem with the all-white juries that refused to convict whites that committed crimes against blacks was not in jury nullification, but in jury selection. The jury was not representative of the community and would not provide a fair and impartial trial.

In recent years, jury nullification has played a role in the trials of Mayor Marion Barry of Washington, DC for drug use, Oliver North for his role in the Iran-Contra Affair, and Bernhard Goetz for his assault in a New York City subway.

In Les Miserables, Victor Hugo highlighted the difference between justice and law. The jury's responsibility is to deliver justice, not to uphold the law. Judges in Maryland and Indiana are required by law to inform the jury of its right to nullification. Article 23 of the Maryland Bill of Rights states:

> "In the trial of all criminal cases, the Jury shall be the judge of Law, as well as of fact, except that the Court may pass upon the sufficiency of the evidence to sustain a conviction."

Nullification applies just as much in other states, including Pennsylvania. Article I of the Constitution of the Commonwealth of Pennsylvania states in Section 6: "Trial by jury shall be as heretofore, and the right thereof remain inviolate." Section 25 states:

> "To guard against transgressions of the high powers which we have delegated, we declare that everything in this article is excepted out of the general powers of government and shall forever remain inviolate."

Taken together, these two sections mean that juries shall have the powers that they had "Heretofore." i. e. when the Constitution was adopted.

Judges usually do not inform the jury of this right. Even worse, some judges instruct the jury that it does not have the right to interpret or nullify the law, but only to determine the facts. The U. S. federal court judges are required to tell this to jurors.

Near the end of alcohol prohibition, juries refused to convict for alcohol violations. Has the time arrived for juries to do the same for marijuana violations?

VI. CRIMINAL COURT OF MANHATTAN

At arraignment, I was assigned orally a court hearing date for June 20, 2007, in the Criminal Court of Manhattan. No explanation of the purpose of this hearing was given, even though I requested it. I agreed to appear at the hearing.

A. INFORMATIONS AND MOTIONS SUBMITTED

I filed several informations and motions with the Criminal Court of Manhattan. The Court did not respond to any of the motions. On May 4, 2007, I moved that the People of New York return my confiscated demonstration signs or reimburse me for the cost of $60.00 plus 6% sales tax. A picture of me holding the signs at the demonstration is shown on page 26.

On May 4, 2007, I notified the Court that I would act as counsel *pro se*. The identity of the presiding judge or prosecuting assistant district attorney was never given to me, either orally or in writing.

On May 4, 2007, I moved that the Court inform me of the nature of the court appearance on June 20, 2007, what information I must be prepared to submit, and what actions may occur.

On May 4, 2007, I moved that the Court order the district attorney to convene a Grand Jury to examine evidence and decide if an indictment is warranted. I quoted Article I, Section 1 §6 of the Constitution of the State of New York, and Amendments V and XIV, Section 1 of the U. S. Constitution to support this request. I also submitted my **BRIEF FOR CONVENING A GRAND JURY** (See Chapter IV of this book) in support of my request on July 2, 2007.

On May 4, 2007. I submitted an information in which I pleaded not guilty and moved that the Court grant a jury trial. I cited Amendment I, Section 1, §2 of the Constitution of the State of New York and Amendments VI and XIV, Section 1 of the U. S. Constitution in support of this motion.

On May 4, 2007, I submitted an information that included the police allegations and informed the Court that perjury will be a major issue at trial. I further notified the Court that I intended to interview any or all persons, individually and privately, who might give testimony at trial.

I moved that the Court order the District Attorney to provide names and contact information for all persons claiming that their pedestrian or vehicular traffic was impeded, or that they were caused inconvenience, annoyance, or alarm. I moved that the Court order the District Attorney to provide names, rank, badge number, and contact information for all persons effecting the arrest, including those persons that received me at police headquarters. I moved that the Court order the District Attorney to provide the name, address, and contact information of the lady who identified herself as a nurse and came to my aid while I was on the ground, and who pleaded with the police not to make the arrest.

I moved that the Court order the District Attorney to provide names, addresses and contact information of any other persons who may testify at my trial. I informed the Court that I might call any of the persons described above as witnesses for the defense, by subpoena, if necessary. I moved that the Court order all persons who will testify at any procedure regarding the case to be sequestered during all proceedings regarding the case, so that they cannot hear the testimony of other testifiers or statements of the District Attorney (or his stand in) or of the Defendant (me).

On May 7, 2007, I requested a writ of *habeas corpus* and moved that the Court dismiss all charges and release the Defendant (me). The request for the writ included information about the arrest, the police allegations, the cause of arrest, and the claims of Defendant.

On May 9, 2007, I moved that the Court order that there be no preliminary hearing.

On May 11, 2007, I submitted a list of questions to the Court about jury selection. I asked:

1. How is the master jury list prepared?
2. What reasons would exclude or permit a person from being on the master jury list?
3. What is the racial, religious, gender, and age composition of persons on the master jury list?
4. How are the persons on the jury pool for *voir dire* chosen?
5. What questions are asked of potential jury pool members before being included in the jury pool for *voir dire*?
6. What reasons would exclude a person from being in the jury pool for *voir dire*?
7. What reasons would permit a potential jury pool member to be excused from being in the jury pool for voir dire?
8. How and when can I get a list of the persons in the jury pool for *voir dire*?

I moved that the Court provide answers to the above questions. I stated that I did not want the persons in the jury pool for *voir dire* to hear the answers of other jury pool members during *voir dire*. I moved that the Court order the members of the jury pool to be sequestered during *voir dire*.

On May 21, 2007, I notified the Court that I had submitted 10 informations with 13 Motions, and that I needed replies to the Motions by June 8, 207, so that I could prepare for the Court date of June 20, 2007. I moved that the Court reply to my Motions before June 8, 2007.

On June 1, 2007, I moved that the Court provide me with a copy of the arraignment transcript of April 18, 2007.

On June 11, 2007, I notified the Court that I would not appear at the hearing of June 20, 2007, because the Court did not respond to any of my requests, and without the information requested, I would not have time to prepare for a Court appearance.

On June 11, 2007, I also filed an Interlocutory Appeal. It included arguments for jurisdiction, standing, causes for action, claims, justifications, and remedy.

B. ACTIONS BY THE CRIMINAL COURT OF MANHATTAN

On June 20, 2007, I was informed by a telephone call from Kenny Fay of the office of the Clerk of Court that the Court issued a bench warrant for my arrest, because I did not appear for the court date.

On June 26, 2007, I filed a motion to quash the bench arrest warrant. In the information provided, I included the information that I had not been committed at arraignment, nor indicted by a Grand Jury. I mentioned that I had filed a notice of appeal with the filing fee of $210 to the Criminal Court of Manhattan. I pointed out that the trial court has no standing to proceed with the trial for four separate and independent reasons. These are:

1. Defendant has not been served with a valid arraignment commitment
2. Defendant has not been indicted by a Grand Jury
3. Defendant has not had a *Habeas Corpus* hearing.
4. Defendant has filed an interlocutory appeal.

In addition I had filed a Petition for a Temporary Restraining Order. I moved that the Court quash the Bench Arrest Warrant issued by the trial court on June 20, 2007.

About a week later, I received a telephone call from Police Detective John Anasa, Shield #4740 (Telephone 516–635–9013) informing me of the bench warrant and asking me to come to a police station to clear the warrant. I did not comply. I have never received nor seen a written document or the name of the issuing judge, if there even is one, indicating that an arrest warrant was issued.

It is apparent from the following that there is no intent to enforce the arrest warrant. Its function solely is harassment and to make it difficult to obtain compensation from the police.

As far as know, extradition papers have not been filed with the state of New Jersey. I have never been contacted by the New Jersey police or sheriffs.

I frequently visit Manhattan and make it a point to talk with police officers. None has ever mentioned the warrant.

I have demonstrated several times in front of the New York Times buildings displaying signs reading: "**STOP HATING JEWS**" and "**N Y TIMES HATES JEWS**." I also distributed literature criticizing the NY Times.

On the first occasion at the New York Times, a security guard ordered me to move away from the wall. I ignored the guard, who then called the police in my presence. I continued my demonstration for about another hour, but the police did not appear.

On subsequent appearances, I have engaged the police and the outside NY times security guard in conversation. No action was taken by the police. The Criminal Court of Manhattan is trying to protect the police officers in their criminal activity, and thus is an accessory to their crimes.

I have filed papers in person twice in the New York State Supreme Court New York County-Civil Branch and appeared twice in the Supreme Court of the State of New York-Appellate Division: First Department. My identity was known to the clerks, but the subject of the warrant was never broached.

On my second visit to the Supreme Court New York County-Civil Branch, I informed the Clerk that I was pursuing a Request for Judicial Intervention (RJI) because there was a bench warrant for my arrest. I was advised by the Clerk to drop the RJI and stay out of New York State. No attempt was made to effect an arrest.

VII. NEW YORK STATE SUPREME COURT

I filed a Request for Judicial Intervention (RJI) with the New York State Supreme Court: New York County-Civil Branch on July 10, 2007, moving for dismissal of the case and quashing the bench warrant on the grounds that I was being denied a fair and speedy trial. Fifteen (15) separate reasons were given in support of these contentions.

The Clerk of the Court said that he would examine the RJI to see if it was proper. I was asked to return the next day, but was unable to return until July 17, 2007.

I returned on July 17, 2007. I then personally delivered the RJI to the secretary of Judge Edward Lehner at 11:45 am. I was informed by the secretary that Judge Lehner was at a funeral and would not return until 2:15 pm. I left the RJI with the secretary and left for lunch.

I returned at 2:00 pm. The room was locked. It was opened at 2:15 pm, and I was notified by a court officer that the judge had just returned. A number of people, including me, were admitted to the court room, where Judge Lehner presided over another case commencing at 2:30 pm.

At about 3:00 pm a court order was given to me by a court officer. Obviously Judge Lehner had failed to read the 100-page RJI, but denied the RJI on July 17, 2007, on the grounds that "...as petitioner has set forth no basis for the relief sought."

I filed a **PETITION FOR RECONSIDERATION** to the Supreme Court of the State of New York, New York County-Civil Branch where the fifteen (15) reasons were repeated. The petition was forwarded by the Clerk of the New York State Supreme Court, New York County-Civil Branch to the Supreme Court of the State of New York-Appellate Division: First Department, which returned it to me.

A **NOTICE OF APPEAL** was filed with the the Supreme Court of the State of New York, New York County-Civil Branch on August 11, 2007.

I tried to file a **LEAVE TO APPEAL OF REFUSAL OF THE REQUEST FOR JUDICIAL INTERVENTION** (RJI) to the Supreme Court of the State of New York-Appellate Division: First Department on August 16, 2007, but it was rejected because it was necessary to file a motion for leave to appeal first.

I filed a **MOTION FOR LEAVE TO APPEAL** with the Supreme Court of the State of New York-Appellate Division: First Department on August 27, 2007, along with the filing fee of $45.00. A response date of September 26, 2007, and time of 10:00 am was requested.

I appeared at the Court on September 26, 2007, at 9:45 am, but was informed by the Clerk's office that I was not permitted to attend the hearing, and that I would be notified by mail of the Court's decision in 2-4 weeks. I left a self-addressed envelope for the reply.

On November 27, 2007, the Supreme Court of the State of NY, Appellate Division: First Department denied my application pursuant to CPLR 5704(a), which states:

> "§5704. Review of *ex parte* orders. (a) By appellate division. The appellate division or a justice thereof may vacate or modify any order granted without notice to the adverse party by any court or a judge thereof from which an appeal would lie to such appellate division; and the appellate division may grant any order or provisional remedy applied for without notice to the adverse party and refused by any court or a judge thereof from which an appeal would lie to such appellate division."

To me, CPLR 5704(a) means that the appellate division "may vacate or modify any order granted without notice to the adverse party..." Therefore the appellate division denied hearing the motion for no valid reason.

I have not filed an appeal with the State of New York Court of Appeals, because two lower courts have denied relief for invalid reasons. Furthermore CPLR 5611 states, in part:

> "If the appellate division disposes of all the issues in the action its order shall be considered a final one, and a subsequent appeal may be taken only from that order and not from any judgment or order entered pursuant to it."

There is no reason to believe that the State of New York Court of Appeals will behave any differently than the other New York State courts.

VIII. NEW YORK CITY COMPTROLLER

In New York there is a requirement that claims against New York City be sent to the Comptroller for adjudication before suing in court. General Municipal Law §50(e) is a New York City statute requiring that a claimant provide specific information about a claim within ninety days of its occurrence. I have submitted four (4) separate claims to the Comptroller of the City of New York. These are:

2007PI018759 & 2007PD018761: Claim against NY City police, mailed June 27, 2007
2007PI023947: Claim against Criminal Court of Manhattan, mailed August 22, 2007
2007PI027148: Claim against NY State Supreme Court, New York County-Civil Branch, mailed September 20, 2007
2007LW032284: Claim against Supreme Court of the State of NY- Appellate Division, 1st Department, mailed November 13, 2007

The Comptroller's office assigned identification numbers to the complaints. It closed the case against the Supreme Court of the State of NY: Appellate Division–First Department on December 12, 2007, because it claims that it is not a city agency.

1. Claim Against New York City Police

The claim against the New York City police was for theft of two picket signs and for false arrest. I asked for $96.30 for the replacement costs of the signs and for $50,000 for the false arrest. Enclosed was a picture of the demonstration (See page 26). One of my signs appears in the upper left-hand corner. I described the facts of the arrest.

On July 10, 2007, I received two identical replies from Michael Aaronson, Bureau Chief, Bureau of Law Adjustment. One of these replies assigned claim number 2007PI018759; the other assigned claim number 2007PD018761. However he did not sign either letter. He stated that my claim was currently under investigation. He further stated that:

> "If we are unable for any reason to settle or resolve your claim and you wish to pursue your claim, you may bring a lawsuit against the City, if it is started within one year ninety days from the date of the occurrence."

He also stated:

> "that property damage claims can take several months to investigate because, as part of our investigation, we must obtain necessary reports."

On July 19, 2007, the Comptroller's office sent two forms requesting further information regarding the claim. I responded on August 18, 2007, with the requested information, which included the police allegations.

In a letter of September 16, 2007, Yvonne Roman, Bureau of Law Adjustment notified me that my claim for damages was still under review. She stated that she was waiting receipt of reports from the agency or agencies involved in my claim. She again reminded me that if my claim is not adjusted that I can bring a lawsuit against the City if it is started within one year and ninety days from the date of occurrence. She did not sign her letter.

On April 16, 2008, I received another letter from Yvonne Roman, again unsigned, advising me that if my claim is unresolved, I can bring a lawsuit against the City. I never heard further from the Comptroller's office about this claim.

2. Claim Against the Criminal Court of Manhattan

On August 22, 2007, I filed a claim against the Criminal Court of Manhattan. I claimed that I was denied a fair and speedy trial, that I was not committed by arraignment nor indicted by Grand Jury. I stated that I was assigned a court date of June 20, 2007, but not notified why. I was denied a *habeas corpus* hearing. An illegal bench warrant was issued. The Court refused to return $210.00 that I had sent by mistake.

My claim was for $210.00 for the unreturned money plus $50,000 and court costs for damages. On September 11, 2007, Michael Aaronson, Bureau Chief, Bureau of Law and Adjustment sent me the form letter acknowledging receipt of my claim and assigning a claim number of 2007PI023847. Again the letter was not signed. In a follow up letter of September 13, 2007, the Comptroller's office requested information on the date that I became aware that I was not receiving a speedy trial. I responded that the date was June 8, 2007. I never heard further from the Comptroller's office about this claim.

3. Claim Against the New York State Supreme Court: New York County–Civil Branch

On September 20, 2007, I filed a claim against the New York State Supreme Court: New York County–Civil Branch because it refused to consider my Request for Judicial Intervention (RJI). The judge's reason in the **COURT ORDER** ("...as petitioner has set forth no basis for the relief sought.") for denying the the RJI was in conflict with the facts since 15 reasons were given in Exhibit A of the RJI.

In addition I paid $95.00 of the $305.00 filing fee to the Court specifically to have the judge read the RJI. As described in the preceding chapters, the judge could not have read the document in the 15 minutes he had possession.

I requested damages of $50,000.00 plus the filing fee of $295.00 plus costs. Michael Aaronson, Bureau Chief, Bureau of Law and Adjustment, replied with the form letter and assigned a claim number of 2007PI027148. Again the letter was not signed.

No further correspondence was ever received from the Comptroller's office about this claim.

4. Claim Against the New York State Supreme Court: Appellate Division: First Department

On November 13, 2007, I filed a claim against the New York State Supreme Court: Appellate Division–First Department for breach of contract and denial of constitutional right to redress in the courts of the State of New York. I requested $50,000.00 in damages plus $45.00 filing fee plus other costs. A long brief accompanied my claim.

On December 7, 2007, I received a short note from Michael Aaronson acknowledging receipt of the claim and assigning a claim number of 2007LW032284. Again the letter was unsigned.

On December 12, 2007, I received a short note from Evelyn Cornick, Claims specialist, Law division, Room 1200, advising me that the Supreme Court of the State of New York–Appellate Division is not an agency of the City of New York. Thus the Comptroller's office was closing the claim. This letter was signed, the only time the Comptroller's office sent a signed response.

5. Deniability

Most of the state officials refuse to sign any documents, so that they can retain deniability. Specific examples follow:

The identities of the prosecuting Assistant District Attorney and the trial Judge have not been divulged. Neither of them has submitted copies of any documents to me, including the alleged bench arrest warrant.

On Judge Lehner's ORDER from the New York State Supreme Court, New York County-Civil Branch, some chicken scratching appears over the word "signature," but the Judge's printed name is nowhere near the chicken scratching and is barely legible.

The **ORDER** of the Supreme Court of the State of New York, Appellate Division: First Department is not signed by any judge, but by the Clerk of Court. The Clerk is not empowered to issue Court orders, so the judges can deny responsibility for the **ORDER**.

Most of the correspondence from the Comptroller's office is unsigned, so that they are worthless legal documents. The failure to sign documents is the behavior of people who know that they are doing wrong.

IX. SUIT FOR DAMAGES TO U. S. DISTRICT COURT

On January 11, 2008, I submitted a Complaint to the United States District Court for the Southern District of New York entitled **PETITION FOR RELIEF TO STOP PROSECUTION**. All the Exhibits and supporting documents were enclosed. The list of Defendants was:

Raymond Kelley, New York City Police Commissioner
Jason Toala, Police Officer, Shield 27613
John Does 1, 2, and 3, Arresting Police Officers, NYSID 2569223LI
Robert M. Morgenthau, District Attorney, New York County
John Doe 4, Assistant District Attorney for Criminal Case #2007NY029913
Honorable Eileen Koretz, Supervising Judge, Criminal Court of Manhattan
Serena Springle, Borough Chief Clerk, Criminal Court of Manhattan
John Doe 5, Judge issuing bench arrest warrant for Julian Heicklen, Docket #2007–NY029913
Jaqueline W. Silbermann, Administrative Judge, New York State Supreme Court, New York County-Civil Branch
Honorable Norman Goodman, County Clerk, New York State Supreme Court, New York County-Civil Branch
Justice Edward Lehner, New York State Supreme Court, New York County-Civil Branch
Jonathon Lippman, Presiding Judge, Supreme Court of the State of New York-Appellate Division: First Department
Richard T. Andrias, Justice, Supreme Court of the State of New York-Appellate Division: First Department

George D. Marlow, Justice, Supreme Court of the State of New York-Appellate Division: First Department
John T. Buckley, Justice, Supreme Court of the State of New York-Appellate Division: First Department
James M. Catterson, Justice, Supreme Court of the State of New York-Appellate Division: First Department
John McConnell, Chief Clerk, Supreme Court of the State of New York-Appellate Division: First Department
Honorable Judith S. Kaye, Chief Judge of the State of New York
William C. Thompson, Jr., Comptroller of the City of New York
Michael Aaronson, Bureau Chief, Bureau of Law and Adjustment, Comptroller's Office of New York City
Yvonne Roman, Bureau of Law and Adjustment, Comptroller's Office of New York City
Scott M. Springer, Manhattan Borough President
Michael Bloomberg, Mayor of New York City
Elliott Spitzer, Governor of New York State

1. Constitutional Issues

I mentioned that several U. S. Constitution issues were involved. These are:

> U. S. Constitution, Amendment I: "Congress shall make no law ...prohibiting the right of the people peaceably to petition the Government for a redress of grievances."
>
> U. S. Constitution, Amendment IV: "The right of the people to be secure in their persons, houses, papers, and effects, against unreasonable searches and seizures, shall not be violated,...:"
>
> U. S. Constitution, Amendment V: "No person shall be held to answer for a capital, or otherwise infamous crime, unless on a presentment or indictment of a Grand Jury,...nor be deprived of life, liberty or property without the due process of law;"

U. S. Constitution, Amendment VI: "In all criminal prosecutions, the accused shall enjoy the right to a speedy and public trial, by an impartial jury of the State and district wherein the crime shall have been committed;..."

U. S. Constitution, Amendment VII: "In Suits at common law, where the value in controversy shall exceed twenty dollars, the right of trial by jury shall be preserved,..."

U. S. Constitution, Amendment VIII: "Excessive bail shall not be required,..."

U. S. Constitution, Amendment XIV, Section 1: "...nor shall any State deprive any person of life, liberty, or property, without the process of law; nor deny to any person within its jurisdiction the equal protection of the laws."

U. S. Constitution, Article I, Section 9..."The Privilege of the Writ of Habeas Corpus shall not be suspended, unless when in cases of Rebellion or Invasion the public Safety require it."

2. Pertinent History

I included a section on the pertinent history, which has been given in detail earlier in this book. This included my experiences with and submissions to the police, the Criminal Court of Manhattan, The New York State Supreme Court: New York County–Civil Branch, the Supreme Court of the State of New York- Appellate Division: First Department, and the Comptroller of the City of New York.

3. Claims

I included the following claims:

I was arrested illegally on April 17, 2007. The police officers were made aware that the arrest was illegal.

Two (2) picket signs owned and held by me were confiscated by the police and never returned.

I was arraigned on April 18, 2007, but was not committed.

As far as I know, no Grand Jury has been impaneled to decide if an indictment is warranted.

The failure of the Criminal Court of Manhatten to identify the arraignment magistrate, the prosecuting Assistant District Attorney, and the trial Judge; and to give no reason for the court date of June 20, 2007, is not appropriate in a court of law. It is reminiscent of a court of inquisition.

I have been denied my constitutional right to a *habeas corpus* hearing.

I have been denied my constitutional right to a fair and speedy trial.

The bench arrest warrant is not justified, since I have neither been committed nor indicted. The failure of the Court to enforce the bench arrest warrant indicates that there is no intent to bring Plaintiff to trial, but only to harass Plaintiff and make it difficult for him to obtain a redress of grievances in other courts and with the Comptroller of the City of New York.

The failure of the Criminal Court of Manhattan to refund the $210 it mistakenly received from me, unless the Plaintiff appears in court, is using the money as bail. No judge has issued an order for bail money. Thus keeping the $210 is an act of theft.

Justice Edward Lehner of the New York State Supreme Court, New York County-Civil Branch did not read the RJI in spite of the fact that I paid a fee of $95 specifically for that purpose. Justice Lehner denied the RJI because "........as petitioner has set forth no basis for the relief sought.", in spite of the fact that 15 causes of action were given. The **ORDER** of Justice Lehner (Exhibit 1) is not consistent with the facts.

Because the **ORDER** from the Supreme Court of the State of New York-Appeals Division: First Department, is based on a misinterpretation of CPLR 5704(a), I have been denied my constitutional right to redress in the courts of the State of New York, as given in:

a. New York State Constitution, Article I, Section 1. "No member of this state shall be disfranchised, or deprived of any of the rights or privileges secured to any citizen thereof, unless by the law of the land, or the judgment of his or her peers,..." and
b. New York State Constitution, Article I, Section 1 §11. "No person shall be denied the equal protection of the laws of this state or any subdivision thereof. "
c. A denial of equal protection under the law as required by Amendment XIV, Section 1 of the U. S. Constitution.

Claims for damages to the Comptroller of the City of New York have been ignored.

4. Causes of Action

Several Causes for Action were given. These were:

On July 10, 2007, Petitioner filed a Request for Judicial Intervention Index Number 07103459 (Julian Heicklen against Criminal Court of Manhattan). On July 17, 2007, Justice of the Supreme Court Lehner: "ordered that this application for an order to show cause is denied as petitioner has set forth no basis for the relief sought." On the contrary, I had set forth in the Exhibits accompanying the RJI many bases for the relief sought. Specifically, these are:

Item 24 of Exhibit A states: "Police confiscated Petitioner's property and have failed to return it. The Petitioner moved that the Court order the police to return the property or provide compensation (Exhibit G). That motion has been ignored."

Item 25 of Exhibit A states: "At arraignment, Petitioner was not informed of the names of the arraignment magistrate or the prosecuting Assistant District Attorney. Petitioner filed a motion to obtain the name of the arraignment magistrate (Exhibit H), but it was ignored by the Court."

Item 26 of Exhibit A states: "At arraignment, Petitioner was not informed of the case Docket Number."

Item 27 of Exhibit A states: "The arraignment commitment form was not signed by a judge or anyone else (Exhibit B). It is not a valid document."

Item 28 of Exhibit A states: "The arraignment magistrate had not even looked at the arraignment commitment document. This became apparent when the Petitioner asked for a jury trial. The arraignment magistrate had to ask the Assistant District Attorney what the charges were against Petitioner to see if he qualified for a jury trial."

Item 29 of Exhibit A states: "Petitioner informed the Court that he would serve as counsel *pro se* (Exhibit I). Neither the Court nor the District Attorney has notified Petitioner of the names of the officiating judge or the prosecuting Assistant District Attorney."

Item 30 of Exhibit A states: 'The failure of the Court to inform Petitioner of the identity of any of the officials involved in his case is not the way a court of law should operate. It is the modus operandi of a court of inquisition. It shows disdain for the accused, thus precluding the possibility of an impartial trial."

Item 31 of Exhibit A states: "A court date was set for June 20, 2007. Petitioner cleared his calendar and notified the Court that he would be available all day, if necessary (Exhibit J)."

Item 32 of Exhibit A states: "Petitioner moved that the Court inform him of the nature of the court appearance, what information must be submitted, and what actions may occur (Exhibit J). There was no response to the motion. Apparently, the Court felt it proper for the accused to be uninformed, so that he could not defend himself adequately."

Item 67 of Exhibit A states: "As a result of the non-response, Petitioner notified the Court that he would not appear at the court date of June 20, 2007 (Exhibit D)."

Item 34 of Exhibit A states: "Petitioner requested a Grand Jury hearing at the arraignment. He also so moved that the Court order the District Attorney to convene a Grand Jury to examine the evidence and decide if an indictment was warranted (Exhibit K). That request and motion were ignored."

Item 35 of Exhibit A states: "There is a widespread misconception in the trial courts that a Grand Jury indictment is not required for misdemeanor offenses. This is not true, as shown in my **BRIEF FOR CONVENING A GRAND JURY** (Exhibit L)."

Item 36 of Exhibit A states: "Petitioner requested at the arraignment that the Court grant a jury trial and so moved in petition to the Court (Exhibit M). The arraigning magistrate granted the jury trial, but the Court gave no response and ignored the motion."

Item 37 of Exhibit A states: "In his petition on **TESTIMONY** (Exhibit N), Petitioner moved that the Court order the District Attorney to provide names and contact information for all witnesses, arresting officers, the lady who identified herself as a nurse and interceded on behalf of Petitioner, and any other persons who may testify at Petitioner's trial. No response. Motions ignored."

Item 38 of Exhibit A states: "Petitioner moved that the Court order all persons who will testify at any proceedings regarding the case be sequestered during all proceedings (Exhibit N). No response. Motion ignored."

Item 39 of Exhibit A states: "Petitioner filed a **WRIT OF *HABEAS CORPUS*** and asked to drop all charges (Exhibit O). No response. Motion ignored."

Item 40 of Exhibit A states: "Petitioner moved that there be no preliminary hearing (Exhibit P). No response. Motion ignored."

Item 41 of Exhibit A states: "Petitioner filed a request concerning the trial jury (Exhibit Q). He moved that the Court provide information about jury selection and that the jury pool be sequestered during jury selection. No response. Motions ignored."

Item 42 of Exhibit A states: "Petitioner requested a reply date to his motions of June 8, 2007, so that he could prepare for the court date of June 20, 2007 (Exhibit R). No response. Motion ignored."

Item 43 of Exhibit A states: "Petitioner moved that the Court provide him with a copy of the arraignment transcript of April 18, 2007 (Exhibit S). No response. Motion ignored."

Item 44 of Exhibit A states: "**The INTERLOCUTORY APPEAL OF JUNE 11, 2007** (Exhibit C) sent to the trial court was ignored and disregarded."

Item 45 of Exhibit A states: "Petitioner was notified on June 20, 2007, that a bench arrest warrant was issued, because petitioner did not appear at the court appearance scheduled for that day."

Item 46 of Exhibit A states: "Petitioner has filed MOTION TO QUASH BENCH ARREST WARRANT (Exhibit T). No response. Motion ignored."

5. Damages Sought

The damages claimed were:

I was held in police custody for 22 hours on April 17–18, 2007, with attendant anxiety and shame.

Police confiscated two (2) picket signs on April 17, 2007, whose replacement cost was $96.30.

I was neither committed nor indicted. Yet a bench arrest warrant was issued when I did not appear for an unexplained court hearing on June 20, 2007. I have been a fugitive from justice since

June 20, 2007, with attendant anxiety, shame, and bitterness. I have had many sleepless nights.

I have been denied Grand Jury and *habeas corpus* hearings, leading to attendant anxiety and frustration.

The courts have ignored my efforts to defend myself, thus leading to anxiety, frustration, and bitterness.

The Criminal Court of Manhattan has withheld $210.00 of my money. This is an act of theft.

I have lost filing fees of $305.00 to the Supreme Court of New York County-Civil Branch, $45.00 to the Supreme Court of New York-Appeals Division: First District, and $350.00 to the U. S. District Court of New York City.

I have spent a significant amount of time and money since April 17, 2007, learning New York State laws and the procedures of the various courts, preparing court documents, and traveling back and forth to New York courthouses.

I have incurred expenses of printing, copying, and mailing court documents and Claims to the Comptroller of the City of New York. There is no reason to believe that the State of New York Court of Appeals will behave any differently than the other New York State courts.

6. Remedies Sought

The remedies sought were:

I moved that the U. S. District Court for the Southern District of New York drop the charges against me and dismiss the case. This can be done by a permanent restraining order on the Criminal Court of Manhattan.

I moved that the U. S. District Court for the Southern District of New York quash the bench arrest warrant against me.

I moved that I be compensated for all court associated costs and out-of-pocket expenses listed above.

I moved that I be compensated for time spent learning New York and federal law and court procedures and in preparing court documents.

I moved that I be compensated for anxiety, shame, bitterness, and sleepless nights resulting from the arrest of April 17, 2007, and the bench arrest warrant of June 20, 2007.

I moved that I be compensated for the the failure of the courts to provide a fair and speedy trial.

I moved for a jury trial as guaranteed by the U. S. Constitution, Amendment VII, which states, in part: "In Suits at common law, where the value in controversy shall exceed twenty dollars, the right of trial by jury shall be preserved,..."

X. OPINION OF JUDGE WOOD

On March 11, 2008, Chief Judge Kimba M. Wood of the United States District Court, Southern District of New York filed an **OPINION** in response to my Complaint. For the reasons that follow, I was directed to submit an amended complaint.

Judge Wood rejected my requests to intervene in the ongoing criminal proceedings against me. She referred to previous U. S. Supreme Court decisions [Younger v. Harris, 401 U. S. 37 (1971) and Gibson v. Berryhill, 411 U. S. 564, 573–74 (1973)], as well as Diamond "D" Const. Corp v. McGowan, 282 F.3d 191, 198 (2nd Cir. 2002) which "requires federal courts to abstain from taking jurisdiction over federal constitutional claims that involve or call into question ongoing state proceedings." She further states: "To the extent plaintiff asks this Court to intervene in ongoing criminal proceedings against him in state court, the claim is dismissed as he fails to allege facts demonstrating that the criminal proceedings pending against him present special circumstances of bad faith, harassment or irreparable injury meriting this Court's intervention. Gibson, 411 U. S. at 573–74."

Apparently Judge Wood does not believe that bad faith or harassment occurs if criminal court officials fail to identify themselves, if a person is ordered into a court hearing without explaining its nature, when he has neither been indicted nor committed, if the court does not respond to submitted informations, if the court ignores a request for a *habeas corpus* hearing, if the court refuses to return $210 sent in error, and if the court issues an arrest warrant. Furthermore she does not consider it to be bad faith if a judge falsifies an **ORDER** in response to a **REQUEST FOR JUDICIAL INTERVENTION**. Also, apparently she is not concerned if the New York State Supreme Court–Appellate Division: First Department violates its own rules when reaching a decision on allowance of a leave for appeal. Presumably all of these are permitted procedures in federal court as well.

In fact there is no ongoing criminal case against me. New York State has had opportunities to arrest me, but neglected to do so. The courts have washed their hands of my case, since no jury would convict me, and the prosecution witnesses would be guilty of perjury. The purpose of the arrest warrant is to give the appearance that the case is ongoing in order to protect the police and the court officials.

1. Judicial Immunity

Judge Wood cites several cases that uphold that: "Judges have absolute immunity for judicial acts performed in their Judicial capacities." "This absolute 'judicial immunity is not overcome by allegations of bad faith or malice," nor can a judge 'be deprived of immunity because the action he took was in error...or was in excess of his authority." The latter quote is from a ruling in Mireles, 502 U. S. at 12–13 (quoting Stump, 45 U. S. at 356). She dismissed my claims against all the judges.

The jurisdiction of the U. S. federal courts in this case is based on statute 42 U.S.C. §1983 which states:

> "Every person who, under color of any statute, ordinance, regulation, custom, or usage, of any State or Territory or the District of Columbia, subjects, or causes to be subjected, any citizen of the United States or other person within the jurisdiction thereof to the deprivation of any rights, privileges, or immunities secured by the Constitution and laws, shall be liable to the party injured in an action at law, suit in equity, or other proper proceeding for redress, except that in any action brought against a judicial officer for an act or omission taken in such officer's judicial capacity,

> injunctive relief shall not be granted unless a declaratory decree was violated or declaratory relief was unavailable. For the purposes of this section, any Act of Congress applicable exclusively to the District of Columbia shall be considered to be a statute of the District of Columbia."

A comprehensive discussion of this statute with court rulings is given by Ian D. Forsythe (http://www.constitution.org/brief/forsythe_42-1983.htm). The immunity clause in this statute is good law. Judges are human and will make honest mistakes. If they could be sued every time they made a mistake, it would be impossible for them or the courts to function. That is why we have appeal courts—to rectify the mistakes. If a judge's ruling is subject to appeal and is reviewed, he should be immune from prosecution, as stated in 42 U.S.C. §1983.

However it is a different situation if injunctive relief is not available. Then 42 U.S.C. §1983 does not grant immunity. In my case three attempts to appeal were rebuffed (RJI, Petition for Reconsideration, and Request for Leave to Appeal). Therefore the judges should not be immune from prosecution.

With regard to Judges Goodman, Koretz, Silberman, and Chief Judge Judith Kaye, I did not include allegations detailing how these defendants violated any federal rights. Charges against them were also dismissed, since they were *respondeati superior* and did not participate in any of the alleged acts. My reason for including them was that the infractions of their underlings were extensive and probably routine. If so, they must have been aware of them and took no action to prevent their reoccurrence. In that instance they would share guilt.

Judith S. Kaye, Chief Judge of the State of New York, retired at the end of 2008. The New York Times (News of the Week in Review, Sunday, December 14, 2008, page 9) wrote a glowing editorial about her. If Judge Kaye represents the best that our judiciary can provide, then armed rebellion is the only solution. However I know several people, none of whom are lawyers, who would never allow a court system to function as improperly as the New York courts.

2. Prosecutorial Immunity

Judge Wood dismissed the complaints against District Attorney Robert Morgenthau and the assistant district attorney prosecuting the case on the grounds that prosecutors like judges are immune from civil suits where the acts were "intimately associated with the judicial phase of the criminal process..." and she cited several court decisions to support her action (Imbler v. Pachtman, 424 U. S. 409,430 (1976); Buckley v. Fitzsimmons, 509 U.S.259 (1993); Burns v. Reed, 500 U. S. 478 (1991); Hill v. City of New York, 45 F.3d 653,660 (2d Cir. 1995); Dory v. Ryan, 25 F.3d 81 (2d Cir. 1994); Schloss v. Bouse, 876 F.2d 287 (2d Cir. 1989); Taylor v. Kavanagh, 640 F.2d 450,452 (2d Cir.1981); and Lee v. Willins, 617 F.2d 320 (2d Cir.). However these decisions are not applicable here because "injunctive relief was not available."

Moreover, Judge Wood argued that District Attorney Morganthau cannot be held liable because he is a *respondeat superior*. However, it is my contention that he has been aware of his assistant district attorneys' improper behavior and has condoned, or at least permitted it. If so, he is not a *respondeat superior*, but is implicated in the improper activities of his employees.

3. Clerk of Court

Judge Wood dismissed the claim against the Clerk of the Criminal Court of Manhattan on the grounds that there were no constitutional issues involving him. Therefore he was immune from prosecution in a federal court.

4. Return of Property

Judge Wood dismissed the claim for loss of property on the grounds that it was a state matter, and that the federal courts have no jurisdiction.

5. False Arrest

Judge Wood stated that plaintiff failed to allege that the arresting officers did not have probable cause to arrest him. New York Penal Law §240.20 states:

> "A person is guilty of disorderly conduct when, with intent to cause public inconvenience or alarm, or recklessly creating a risk thereof:...(5) [h]e obstructs vehicular or pedestrian traffic; or (6) [h]e congregates with other persons in a public place and refuses to comply with a lawful order of the police to disperse..."

Judge Wood stated that I failed to state that I was arrested without probable cause. However she granted leave to file an amended complaint detailing allegations that I was arrested without probable cause.

> "If plaintiff chooses to file an amended complaint, he is therefore directed to include allegations regarding whether or not he was convicted of any charges with respect to the April 17, 2007 arrest or, if not, whether any charges remain pending against him."

Judge Wood's last request is catch 22, There are charges remaining against me, but I have not been committed nor indicted, and the Criminal Court of Manhattan has no intention of resolving the matter. In this way, the Criminal Court of Manhattan essentially has dismissed the case, but protected all individuals from legal action against them.

6. Conclusion

Judge Woods instructions were:

> "Plaintiff is hereby directed to file an amended complaint containing the information specified above. Plaintiff should not include in the amended complaint those defendants and claims that have been dismissed."
>
> "The Court certifies pursuant to 28 U.S.C. §1915(a)(3) that any appeal from this order would not be taken in good faith. See Coppedge v. United States, 369 U. S. 438, 444–45 (1962)"

I was denied several Constitutional rights and legal redress. I was suing under 42 U.S.C. §1983 for damages and relief. The immunity provisions of 42 U.S.C. §1983 are not applicable, because declaratory relief was unavailable to me. 42 USC 1983 appears on pp. 71-72.

XI. NEW COMPLAINT VS. "IMMUNIZED" ENTITIES

Because of Judge Wood's statement "that any appeal from this order would not be taken in good faith," I decided to file a separate complaint against the disallowed defendants. I indicated that it was improper for a judge to threaten a litigant for exercising his legal rights. I asked that Judge Wood be recused. The revised complaint was given to Judge Harold Baer.

Judge Baer did not consider, or even refer to, any of the claims made in Appellant's **PETITION FOR DAMAGES FOR DEPRIVATION OF RIGHTS.** Judge Baer referred to the **OPINION** by Judge Kimba Wood in District Court S.D.N.Y. Case #08 Civ. 2457 (KMW). Three reasons were given by Judge Wood for dismissal. These are:

a. Some of the Defendants are exempt because of the immunity clause in 42 U.S.C. §1983.
b. Some of the Defendants are exempt because they are *respondeati superior*.
c. Some of the Defendants are exempt because they did not violate a federal law or right.

<u>1. Immunity</u>

In all but one of the court cases regarding judicial immunity discussed by Judge Wood, declaratory relief was available, so that the immunity clause was applicable for those cases.

The case of Huminski v. Corsones et al. 396 F.3d 53 (2d Cir. 2005) was the one case where the immunity clause was relevant. Judge Nancy Corsones ordered Scott Huminski to remove his motor vehicle from the court parking lot during a case in progress because of signs on the vehicle.

Huminski argued that this violated his rights under the First Amendment of the U. S. Constitution. Judge Corsones enforced her decision immediately, so that Huminski had no recourse to judicial review and lost his rights.

Huminski sued Corsones. The U. S. District Court ruled in Huminski's favor, because it decided that Corsones had acted in her executive capacity, not her judicial capacity. On appeal, the U. S. Circuit Court concluded that Judge Corsones had acted in her judicial capacity and reversed the decision.

Both courts were in error. It is irrelevant in which capacity Judge Corsones was acting. The issue, which neither court considered, was the availability of judicial relief. Judicial relief was not available to Huminski. He should have received a favorable judgment. He was denied justice.

I did not challenge the law, of which I approve. I argued that Huminski did not have the opportunity of judicial relief, and therefore the immunity clause was not operative.

In my lawsuit, presumably the Defendants would have argued that judicial relief was available, and the immunity clause is operative. This will be a dispute of fact, not of law. It is not a judge's prerogative to decide facts. That is the duty of the jury. Furthermore another reason for a judge not to decide the facts in this case is that judges have an enormous conflict of interest.

2.*Respondiati Superior*

Four of the Defendants were *respondeati superio*r. These were Robert M. Morgenthau, District Attorney, New York County; William C. Thompson, Jr., Comptroller, Comptroller's Office of New York City; Honorable Eileen Koretz, Supervising Judge, Criminal Court, New York County; and Jacqueline W. Silbermann, Administrative Judge, New York State Supreme Court, New York County-Civil Branch, 1st Judicial District. Ordinarily *respondeati superior* are not liable for prosecution because of improper actions of their subordinates, unless they have directly contributed to the improprieties. I claimed that all four *respondeati superior* were liable.

The Assistant District Attorney at the arraignment attempted to strike a deal with me, if I would agree not to sue the police and not get arrested for 6 months. It is the duty of the District Attorney to prosecute crime, not to defend the criminal actions of police officers. No Assistant District Attorney would take such action if it were not department policy. Therefore I argued that the District Attorney is directly involved and not exempt from prosecution.

The Comptroller's office assigned case numbers to three complaints that I filed, but dismissed a fourth case for lack of jurisdiction. Two different employees (Michael Aaronson and Yvonne Roman) responded to the complaints. Neither signed the correspondence. I never heard from them again concerning the outcome of the complaints. Obviously, the Comptroller's office is under instructions to ignore complaints and let them die, so as to discourage victims from filing court cases. Instead of helping victims solve their problems, the Comptroller's office is part of the network to deny justice to victims.

The Chief Judges of the two courts certainly must be aware of how their courts are operating, and have done nothing to remedy the outrages perpetrated by the courts on litigants. If the Chief Judges are not aware, they have been criminally negligent in their duties.

Again, I emphasizes that I was not challenging the law. I was arguing the facts. It is the duty of the jury, not a judge to decide the facts. If I am wrong, a jury will exonerate the Defendants.

3. No violation of a federal law or right

If defendants violate both federal and state laws, the U. S. courts have jurisdiction over both. However if there is no violation of federal law, then the U. S. courts have no jurisdiction. The case must be argued in a state court. The U. S. District Court claimed that some defendants did not violate a federal law or right. Therefore, it had no jurisdiction.

I claimed that all the defendants violated 42 U. S. C. 1983, which disallows any actors from violating my Constitutional right to freedom of assembly to protest grievances. The Court disagreed. Again, I claimed that this is question of fact, not law, and should be decided by a jury, not a judge.

4.Decision of Judge Baer

Judge Baer did not consider, or even refer to, any of the claims made in my **PETITION FOR DAMAGES FOR DEPRIVATION OF RIGHTS**. Judge Baer referred to the **OPINION** by Judge Kimba Wood in District Court S.D.N.Y. Case #08 Civ. 2457 (KMW) (See Appendix).

Based on Judge Wood's arguments, Judge Baer dismissed my claim. Furthermore, he stated in his decision that an appeal by Appellant would be in bad faith.

XII. APPEAL OF JUDGE BAER'S DECISION

I filed an appeal to the U. S. Court of Appeals: 2nd Circuit based on the following considerations:

1. Decision of Judge Baer

Judge Baer did not consider, or even refer to, any of the claims made in Appellant's **PETITION FOR DAMAGES FOR DEPRIVATION OF RIGHTS**. Judge Baer referred to the **OPINION** by Judge Kimba Wood in District Court S.D.N.Y. Case #08 Civ. 2457 (KMW) (See Appendix).

Three reasons were given by Judge Wood for dismissal. These are:

a. Some of the Defendants are exempt because of the immunity clause in 42 U.S.C. §1983.
b. Some of the Defendants are exempt because they are *respondeati superior*.
c. Some of the Defendants are exempt because they did not violate a federal law or right.

2. Federal Law and Rights

Several of my federal rights were violated. These are:

a. The right to peaceably assemble guaranteed by Amendment I of the U. S. Constitution.
b. The right ".... of the people to be secure in their persons...and no Warrants shall issue, but upon probable cause" as guaranteed by Amendment IV of the U. S. Constitution. An arrest warrant was issued against petitioner when he was neither committed nor indicted for any crime.

c. “In suits at common law...the right of trial by jury shall be preserved” as guaranteed by Amendment VII of the U. S. Constitution.

d. “Excessive bail shall not be required” as guaranteed by Amendment VIII of the U. S. Constitution. Since Appellant was not committed nor indicted, the bail of $210 was excessive—theft actually, since it cannot be recovered.

e. Amendment XIV, Sec 1 of the U. S. Constitution states: “nor shall any State deprive any person of life, liberty, or property without due process of law.”

f. I was kidnapped by the police (a federal offense: 18 U.S.C. §1201) , but was not able to recover damages or receive justice in the New York State courts.

It is the duty of the Comptroller’s and District Attorneys’ offices, as well as the courts to protect citizens from misconduct of the police, not to aid and abet them. All the Defendants named in the instant court case are accessories to the crime, because they did not discharge their duties, but instead acted to defend the criminal actions of the police. I repeated the arguments against immunity and *respondeati superior* given in the previous chapter.

<u>3. Bad Faith</u>

Judge Baer stated in his decision that an appeal by Appellant would be in bad faith. Appellant agrees that bad faith was exhibited here by Judge Baer, not the Appellant. Furthermore Judge Baer threatened Appellant that refiling matters that have been dismissed may result in the imposition of sanctions.

It is outrageous for a court of law to threaten a litigant for exercising his legal rights. Both Judge Baer and Judge Wood have threatened Appellant. They must be recused from trying the instant case.

4. Importance of this Case

This case is not just about an isolated incident of police and judicial malpractice. It is representative of the widespread and ongoing abuse of citizens by the New York City Police and the New York City and State courts. Incidents that Appellant witnessed in these courts involving people who had neither the mental nor financial means to protect themselves were disturbing. These abuses must be stopped.

Furthermore this case is about hate, particularly the hatred of Jews, which is now widespread in the United States and around the world. The police were trying to terminate a peaceful demonstration against the President of Iran. The President of Iran is the modern day reincarnation of Adolph Hitler. He believes the Muslims are the master race, that the state of Israel should be obliterated, and the Jews removed therefrom. He addressed the UN General Assembly several times, where he advocated the destruction of Israel.

I was allowed 5 minutes for oral argument, although I requested at least 30 minutes, but wanted a full day. At oral argument, I barely got through the introductory material. The Defendants did not present an oral argument and were not represented at the oral hearing.

The Court of Appeals affirmed the order of the District Court to dismiss the case without comment.

XIII. REVISED COMPLAINT AGAINST POLICE

The Amended Complaint was mailed to the U. S. District Court, Southern District of New York on April 29, 2008. The defendants named were:

Jason Toala, Police Officer Shield 27613 Patrol Boro Manhattan South Task Force
John Does 1, 2, and 3 Arresting Police Officers Patrol Boro Manhattan South Task Force
Raymond Kelly New York City Police Commissioner
William C. Thompson, Jr. Comptroller of New York City
Michael A. Cardozo Corporation Counsel of New York City

On October 3, 2008, I filed a Petition for *Writ of Mandamus* with the U. S. Court of Appeals: Second Circuit, because I had no response from the District Court. I complained that the District Court was burying the complaint, and I asked for an order to the District Court to proceed. The Court of Appeals denied my request on December 17, 2008. However on January 8, 2009, Judge Harold Baer of the District Court accepted the complaint, but removed William Thompson and Michael Cardozo as Defendants.

On March 2, 2009, Defendants Toala and Kelly were served. On March 19, 2009, Attorney Max McCann filed a **NOTICE OF APPEARANCE** for Raymond Kelly, but not for Jason Toala. He also requested the Court to order me to provide fully executed consents and authorizations.

On March 27, 2009, I replied to Mr. McCann's correspondence of March 19, 2009, in which I stated that:

> "I find it curious that the police have lied to me three times, failed to submit waiver of summons forms, and failed to supply the names of the John Does 1, 2, & 3, but expect me to fulfill their requests. Furthermore Judge Koeltl has failed to act on three motions that I submitted on February 28, 2009. One of these was for a jury trial, a simple request that he cannot deny. A second one was for a time delay for responding to informations submitted in March, 2009, which is now moot. The third motion was to order Defendants Toala and Kelly to provide identification information for the John Does."

On April 2, 2009, Judge Koeltl denied my motions. On April 6, I submitted informations about medical records and the criminal court case to Max McCann with a copy to the Clerk of Court. On April 20, 2009, I sent a notarized statement for designation of agent for access to sealed records. On May 8, 2009, Attorney McMann filed a motion to order me to sign the document prepared by his office. On May 12, 2009, Judge Koeltl issued an **ORDER** for me to provide Defendants the consent and authorization that had been submitted by Attorney McCann.

XIV. WRIT OF *MANDAMUS*

On May 18, 2009, I filed a **PETITION FOR WRIT OF *MANDAMUS*** requesting a **TEMPORARY RESTRAINING ORDER**:

A. PERTINENT HISTORY

Petitioner filed Case # 08–4931–op with the United States Court of Appeals for the Second District on October 3, 2008. Petitioner claimed that the U. S. District Court for the Southern District of New York was burying his Complaint 08 CV 02457. Petitioner asked the Circuit Court to order the District Court to file a case # and proceed with trial.

On December 17, 2008, the Circuit Court **ORDERED** "that the mandamus petition is **DENIED**, without prejudice to renewal if the District Court fails to take action within a reasonable time." On January 8, 2009, Judge Harold Baer, Jr. issued an **ORDER OF PARTIAL DISMISSAL** in which William C. Thompson and Michael Cardozo were removed as Defendants.

However the District Court is still trying to bury this case as indicated:

a. On March 2, 2009, Defendants Toala and Kelly were served with Summons, Amended Complaint, and Plaintiff interrogatories to discover identities and addresses of John Doe Defendants.
b. The Summons states that the answer to the complaint which is served on you with this summons must be filed within 20 days or a judgment by default will be taken against you for the relief demanded in the complaint.

c. No response has been received from Defendant Toala, but the District Court has taken no action. In fact the District Court ignores the existence of Defendant Toala.
d. Two Interrogatories have been submitted to Defendants Toala and Kelly, but they have been ignored.
e. Petitioner filed Motions with the Court to order a response to the Interrogatories. The first was denied by Judge Koeltl. The second was returned to Petitioner by the Clerk of Court with the statement that the Court does not help litigants with discovery.
f. Two other motions submitted by Petitioner to the District Court were denied by Judge Koeltl.
g. A request for information regarding jury selection was submitted by Petitioner to the District Court. It was returned by the Clerk of Court with a statement that the Court does not aid in discovery.
h. Counsel McCann sent an interrogatory (enclosed) to Plaintiff. Plaintiff responded to Mr. McCann on two occasions with modified responses. Copies of both responses were sent to the District Court, but they were returned to Petitioner.
i. Other informations that Petitioner sent to the District Court to be included in the Reproduced Record were returned by the Clerk of Court.

Attorney McCann was not satisfied with either of Petitioner's two responses to the Interrogatory. He filed a Motion with Judge Koeltl to order Petitioner to complete the interrogatory exactly as submitted. On May 9, 2009, Judge Koeltl issued such an ORDER. So much for the Court not aiding in discovery.

There are four reasons why Petitioner is reluctant to complete and return this Interrogatory. These are:

a. The Interrogatory requests Petitioner's social security number. This is not an identity number, and neither the Court nor the Defendants are entitled to it. Furthermore none of the New York State courts have this number, so it is of no legal use to the Defendants.
b. Petitioner has neither been committed nor indicted in the Criminal Court of Manhattan. The arraignment number has been submitted to Attorney McCann several times, as well as all other information relevant to this case.
c. Petitioner does not accept the wording in the document. Twice he has submitted the requested information in his own words to attorney McCann.
d. Petitioner believes that signing the document submitted by Attorney McCann might either tend to incriminate him or be used as evidence against him in the civil trial. He has the right under Amendment V of the U. S. Constitution to avoid the possibility of self incrimination.

Petitioner requests that the Circuit Court issue a **TEMPORARY RESTRAINING ORDER** prohibiting Judge Koeltl from executing his **ORDER** of May 12, 2009. An expanded brief with all Exhibits will be submitted within 30 days requesting a **PERMANENT RESTRAINING ORDER**. Petitioner needs 30 days to respond, because he will be in Richmond, VA from May 18 through May 25 and in Cupertino, CA from June 1 through 9.

B. MOTION

Petitioner moves that the Circuit Court issue a **TEMPORARY RESTRAINING ORDER** prohibiting Judge Koeltl from executing his **ORDER**.

XV. ORDER FOR A HEARING

On June 22, 2009, I wrote the following letter to Judge Koeltl:

I have received your Court **ORDER** of June 16, 2009, to appear for conference on June 26, 2009. I also have received a copy of the letter of June 12, 2009, from Max McCann addressed to you.

There is an inaccuracy in Mr. McCann's letter. He states that Plaintiff "has not provided the undersigned with the executed consent and authorization for the release of records." In fact I responded twice with *carte blanche* permission to contact all of the New York State Courts involved in the issue at hand. Copies of these were submitted to the U. S. District Court, Southern District of New York. The *Pro Se* Clerk of Court returned them to me on April 14, 2009, with the statement that "discovery requests cannot be accepted by the Court." Perhaps you are unaware of this rule, since you sent me an **ORDER** of May 12, 2009, to provide information which I do not have, and which I believe does not exist.

Both you and Mr. McCann have all of my correspondence with all of the New York State courts. It was enclosed with the submission of my **REVISED COMPLAINT** of April 29, 2008. Mr. McCann cleverly convinced you to order me to provide nonexistent information. Since I could not do so, he requested in his letter of June 12, 2009, that you dismiss this case.

In the copy of my letter of June 15, 2009, to the U. S. Circuit Court of Appeals: Second Circuit, I advised the U. S. District Court, Southern District of New York that I would be in Las Vegas, NV, on June 26, 2009. My letter was received by the District Court on June 16, 2009, at 11:39 am. Yet in your **ORDER** of June, 16, 2009, you ordered Mr. McCann and me to appear for a conference on June 26, 2009. Of course I cannot attend on this date. I anticipate that you will find me in contempt of court and dismiss the case.

It is clever of you and Mr. McCann to devise this method of burying this case and protecting the criminal behavior of the police. I now have further substantiation of why the general public holds the legal profession in such low esteem.

In the event that I am wrong in my prediction that you will find me in contempt of court and dismiss this case, I will be pleased to meet with you and Mr. McCann at our mutual convenience. Perhaps we can resolve some or all of the issues that exist. The dates that I am available for court appearances in July and August are:

July 15 after noon
July 16 all day
July 17 after noon
July 22–24 all day
July 27 & 28 all day
July 29 after noon
July 30–31 all day
Aug. 3–6 all day
Aug.18–27 all day
Aug. 28 after noon

I have the financial means to hire an attorney to represent me, but I have chosen to proceed *pro se*. Perhaps I have a fool for a client, but at least I have honest counsel.

Copies of this letter, as well as your **ORDER** of June 16, 2009, and the letter of Mr. McMann of June 12, 2009, are being sent to the U. S. Circuit Court of Appeals: Second Circuit to be included as an **ADDENDUM** to my **AFFIDAVIT FOR WRIT**

OF *MANDAMUS* (CONTINUED): PERMANENT RESTRAINING ORDERS for Circuit Court Case #08-4931-op.

XVI. HEARING OF JULY 17, 2009

THE JUDGE: At the hearing the Defendants suggested that the case be stayed because the criminal case against the Plaintiff remains pending in the state court. And that Defendants suggested, for the protection of the plaintiff's rights, that the case be stayed. So what is the plaintiff's position?

MR. HEICKLEN: Plaintiff's position is that there is no case in the criminal court. The docket number I got was a docket number on the arraignment papers. What happened at the arraignment was that the first thing the magistrate said was before I -- the prosecuting attorney has a plea bargain for you. The plea bargain was, if you plead guilty he will settle for time served, which was one day. I refused on the grounds -- well, I said if I was going to do that, I wouldn't have bothered to get arrested at all. I said I'm pleading not guilty, I want a grand jury hearing, and I want a jury trial.

Neither the counsel for the prosecution nor the magistrate objected to the request for the grand jury hearing or again asked that I plead guilty. The magistrate questioned whether I was entitled to a jury trial, which indicated that she did not know what the case was about. Anyway I said that I was entitled to a -- the DA said I was entitled to a jury trial.

MR. HEICKLEN: I was then given the arraignment papers of which you and Mr. McCann have copies. For your convenience, I have reproduced them again, and I have copies for both of you. Here's one for the Court if you want it. The arraignment papers are underneath here. And the arraignment papers have no magistrate name on it. They are not signed by a magistrate.

MR. HEICKLEN: My claims are against them?

THE JUDGE: Yes.

MR. HEICKLEN: That perjury in fact, when I saw what the claims were, I notified the court that my defense in the criminal case would be perjury of the prosecution's witnesses. That would be my sole defense. Because everything they have stated is a lie. Everything. There isn't one true statement in the claims. I mean, usually I think they would tell some truth. This was just blatant. Let me tell you. You want to hear what happened at the incident and you can see what's going on here. Some of the claims are physically impossible. For one thing, I was standing all alone, they ordered me to join a crowd. One of the charges against me is failure to disperse. If you are standing all alone, how could I disperse? I mean. That is one of the charges failure to disperse. I'm standing all by myself. They ordered me to join a crowd. I refused on the grounds that I had the right to stand there, but there were other reasons as well. That is reckless endangerment ordering me to move into the crowd. Also the crowd was impeding pedestrian traffic. I would have been participating in a crime if I accepted. When I asked them what are the reason you are placing me under arrest, they gave me one reason. "Failure to obey a law of a police officer." That was the only reason they stated at the scene of the crime. They have stated numerous reasons since. As I said, none of them are correct. And many of them were -- are physically impossible.

XVII. DOCUMENTS SUBMITTED

After the hearing, on July 28, 2008, I submitted interrogatories to Mr. McCann to identify the John Doe defendants. In addition, again I submitted access to sealed records:

DESIGNATION OF AGENT FOR ACCESS TO SEALED RECORDS PURSUANT TO NYCPL #160.50[1][d]

"I, Julian Heicklen, born March 9, 1932, pursuant to CPL #160.50[1][d], hereby designate MICHAEL A. CARDOZO, Corporation Counsel of the City of New York, or his authorized representative, as my agent to whom records of the arraignment entitled People of the State of New York v. Julian Heicklen, Misdemeanor Complaint Number 2007NY029913 in the Criminal Court of Manhattan, County of New York, State of New York, relating to my kidnapping on April 17, 2007, may be made available. This includes a copy of the police allegation #750895 signed by Jason Toala, Deponent."

"I understand that until now the aforesaid records have been sealed pursuant to CPL #160.50, which permits that records to be made available only (1) to persons designated by me, or (2) to certain parties specifically designated in that statute. I further understand that the person designated by me above as a person to whom the records may be made available is not bound by the statutory sealing requirements of CPL #160.50."

"The records to be made available to the person designated above comprise all records and related papers relating to my kidnapping in the misdemeanor complaint identified herein on file with any criminal court, police agency, or prosecutors office."

"I submitted documents to the Criminal Court of Manhattan. In addition I filed a **REQUEST FOR JUDICIAL INTERVENTION** and a **REQUEST FOR**

RECONSIDERATION with the New York State Supreme Court, New York County-Civil Branch, Index Number 07103459, and a **LEAVE TO APPEAL** with the Supreme Court of the State of New York, Appellate Division: First Department. Furthermore I filed four Complaints with the New York City Comptroller and a Criminal Complaint with the U. S. Attorney in New York City."

"Both you and the U. S. District Court: Southern District of New York already have copies of all of these documents and the responses. If you wish to verify these with the appropriate agencies, you have my permission to do so."

"There is some information that you requested that I have not supplied. You improperly requested my social security number. U. S. law only requires me to provide this number to collect social security or medicare benefits. Even the Internal Revenue Service is not entitled to know this number. Social Security numbers are not for identification purposes."

"You also requested docket or indictment numbers for the criminal case against me. I do not know that any such numbers exist. There has been no criminal trial. I affirm, under penalty of perjury, that the above is true and correct to the best of my knowledge."

Non-Reply of the Court of Appeals: Second Circuit

I have no evidence that the Court of Appeals: Second circuit ever replied. However Judge Koeltl took no further action, so the issue became moot.

XVIII. THE CRIMINAL NON-TRIAL

On August 6, 2009, I wrote to Judge Koeltl:

"At the hearing of July 17, 2009, it was agreed that Defendants would submit a brief to stay the civil trial until after the criminal trial was completed. I responded that there was no criminal trial. You ordered Defendants to submit a brief supporting their position by July 31, 2009, and that I was to reply by August 14, 2009.

On August 3, 2009, I received Mr. McCann's response. He did not even address the issue of a criminal trial. Nevertheless I am enclosing my response to the question of a criminal trial. You can see from my response that:

1. There never was a criminal trial.
2. There is not now a criminal trial.
3. There never will be a criminal trial.

Since Mr. McCann did not even address this issue, I assume that that my response settles this issue. My response follows:

U. S. DISTRICT COURT:
SOUTHERN DISTRICT OF NEW YORK
Civil Action, File Number llll

THE CRIMINAL NON-TRIAL

A. THE ARRAIGNMENT

The arraignment occurred on April 18, 2007, in the Criminal Court of Manhattan. Neither the arraignment magistrate nor the prosecuting assistant district attorney were identified to the Plaintiff (Defendant in the criminal trial) or to any of the other arrestees in keeping with the procedures of a court of inquisition.

About 15 other arrestees were arraigned before Plaintiff. All of them, except for one man, pleaded guilty. When Plaintiff's turn occurred, the magistrate first asked if he had attended school and, if so, what was his highest degree. Plaintiff, who at the time was 75 years old, responded that he had not attended school recently, but that his highest degree was a Ph. D. in chemistry, and that he was a professor of chemistry. Plaintiff still does not understand why this information was any of the magistrate's business.

Plaintiff was then asked if he had legal counsel. Plaintiff replied that he would be acting as counsel *pro se*. He said that he had tried about 40 cases, but none in New York state. He said that he was unaware of New York laws or court procedures and that he could use an advisory counsel.

At that point the Court appointed Edward McCarthy, Supervising Attorney, Criminal Defense Division, The Legal Aid Society, 100 Centre Street, Room 511, New York, NY 10013 (Telephone: 212 571 5930) as temporary advisory counsel. Coincidentally, the Court had already positioned Mr. McCarthy at Plaintiff's side in the dock.

Plaintiff then was advised by the magistrate that before he pleaded, the prosecuting assistant district attorney had a plea bargain. The prosecuting assistant district attorney offered to settle for time served (22 hours), if Plaintiff would plead guilty.
Plaintiff replied: "If I was willing to accept that, I would not have bothered to be arrested in the first place."

The magistrate asked: "Are you pleading not guilty?" She then warned (threatened) Plaintiff that, if so, he could go to prison. Plaintiff acknowledged that he was aware that a prison sentence was possible. He then pleaded not guilty, demanded indictment by a Grand Jury, and asked for a jury trial.

After the stunned Court recovered, neither the prosecuting assistant district attorney nor the magistrate objected to the plea or the demand for indictment by a Grand Jury. The magistrate had no idea of what the charges were, since she had to ask the prosecuting assistant district attorney if Plaintiff was entitled to a jury trial. The answer was affirmative.

Plaintiff was told that he must report for a court hearing on June 20, 2007, and submit all informations before May 17, 2007. Plaintiff asked the purpose of the hearing, but his question was ignored. No written **ORDER** was issued to appear for the hearing date of June 20, 2007.

Plaintiff was handed the unsigned arraignment form with the police charges and released after 22 hours of confinement. Plaintiff was not committed at arraignment nor at any other time. Plaintiff has not been indicted nor informed that any Grand Jury has been convened.

A few days later, Plaintiff was contacted by Simone Levine, an attorney at The Legal Aid Society, and informed that the prosecuting assistant district attorney was willing to drop the charges and dismiss the case, if Plaintiff would agree to not get arrested in the next 6 months and not sue the police. Plaintiff declined.

It is not clear to Plaintiff why the prosecuting assistant district attorney did not contact Plaintiff directly. It seems to Plaintiff that it is improper for the District Attorney's office to be conducting negotiations with anyone but the Plaintiff.

The function of the District Attorney is to prosecute crime, not to protect it. He should be prosecuting the police, not protecting them. By protecting them, the District Attorney's office is an accessory to the crimes of kidnapping and theft. Both the District Attorney and the prosecuting assistant district attorney should be dismissed from their positions and disbarred.

Plaintiff has filed a complaint against the John Doe assistant district attorney and against District Attorney Robert Morgenthau in the U. S. District Court for the Southern District of New York (Complaint: #09 Civ. 1442 [HB]).

B. THE NON-TRIAL

Plaintiff was assigned orally a court hearing date for June 20, 2007, in the Criminal Court of Manhattan. He agreed to appear at the hearing. [See "Reproduced Record of New York State Supreme Court, New York County-Civil Branch Re: Manhattan Criminal Court Case Docket #2007-NY029913 People of New York against Julian Heicklen." (Hereafter referred to as Reproduced Record) Tab I, Exhibit J, p. 36.]

Plaintiff filed several motions (Reproduced Record, Tab I, Exhibits G-T, pp. 28-100), including a motion for a Grand Jury hearing (Exhibits K and L, pp. 39 and 42), a motion for a jury trial (Exhibit M, p. 50), a motion for a *habeas corpus* hearing (Exhibit O, p. 57) , and a motion for an explanation of the purpose of the court date (Exhibit J, p. 36). The Court did not respond to any of these or other motions.

Plaintiff notified the Court by certified mail on June 11, 2007, that he would not appear at the hearing of June 20, 2007 (Reproduced Record, Tab I, Exhibit D, p. 21). On June 20, 2007, Plaintiff was informed by a telephone call from Kenny Fay from the Clerk of Court that the Court issued a bench warrant for his arrest, because he did not appear for the court date.

About a week later, Plaintiff received a telephone call from Police Detective John Anasa, Shield #4740 (Telephone 516 635 9013) informing him of the bench warrant and asking him to come to a police station to clear the warrant. Plaintiff did not comply.

Plaintiff has never received nor seen a written document or the name of the issuing judge, if there even is one, indicating that an arrest warrant was issued. It is apparent from the following that there is no intent to enforce the arrest warrant. Its function solely is to harass Plaintiff and make it difficult to obtain compensation from the police.

As far as Plaintiff knows, extradition papers have not been filed with the state of New Jersey. Plaintiff has never been contacted by the New Jersey police or sheriffs. Plaintiff frequently visits Manhattan and makes it a point to talk with police officers. None has ever mentioned the warrant.

Plaintiff has filed papers in person twice in the New York State Supreme Court New York County- Civil Branch and appeared twice in the Supreme Court of the State of New York-Appellate Division: First Department. His identity was known to the clerks, but the subject of the warrant was never broached. On his second visit to the Supreme Court New York County-Civil Branch, Plaintiff informed the Clerk that he was pursuing a Request for Judicial Intervention (RJI) because there was a bench warrant for his arrest. Plaintiff was advised by the Clerk to drop the RJI and stay out of New York State. No attempt was made to effect an arrest.

Plaintiff has demonstrated several times in front of the New York Times buildings displaying signs reading: "**STOP HATING JEWS**" and "**N Y TIMES HATES JEWS**." He also distributes literature criticizing the NY Times.

On the first occasion at the New York Times, a security guard ordered Plaintiff to move away from the wall. Plaintiff ignored the guard, who then called the police in Plaintiff's presence. Plaintiff continued his demonstration for about another hour, but the police did not appear. On subsequent appearances, Plaintiff has engaged the police and the outside NY times security guard in conversation. No action by the police.

The Criminal Court of Manhattan is trying to protect the police officers in their criminal activity, and thus is an accessory to their crimes. Plaintiff filed a motion to quash the bench arrest warrant (Reproduced Record, Tab I, Exhibit T, p. 72). The Court did not respond.

On June 11, 2007, Plaintiff filed an interlocutory appeal and a filing fee of $210.00 with the Criminal Court of Manhattan. By two (2) telephone calls from the Clerk's office, Plaintiff was notified that all appeals must be filed with the Supreme Court. In the first call, Plaintiff was told that the the $210.00 would be returned by mail. In the second call, he was notified that the $210.00 would only be returned when he appeared in court.

The identities of the prosecuting assistant district attorney and the trial Judge have not been divulged. Neither of them has submitted copies of any documents to Plaintiff, including the alleged bench arrest warrant.

Plaintiff has received no written documents from the New York County District Attorney's office or the Criminal Court of Manhattan, except for the unsigned arraignment documents.

C. WHY THERE WILL BE NO CRIMINAL TRIAL

Some provisions of New York State Criminal Code CPL 30 are attached as an Exhibit. 43. CPL 30 #30.30 Speedy trial; time limitations 1.b states:

> "ninety days of the commencement of a criminal action wherein a defendant is accused of one or more offenses, at least one of which is a misdemeanor punishable by a sentence of imprisonment of more than three months and none of which is a felony."

This condition has not been met as more than 27 months have passed since the accusation, and a trial has not commenced.

Plaintiff has been denied a speedy criminal trial (within 90 days of accusation) as required by CPL 30 #30.30 (1.b).

Plaintiff has not received an appearance ticket notifying him of his right to receive a supporting deposition, as required by CPL 30 #150.10 (2). CPL 30 #150.60 permits the Court to only issue a warrant of arrest if the accused does not appear at the time the appearance ticket is returnable. Since no appearance ticket was issued, the warrant of arrest is illegal, and makes the Criminal Court of Manhattan an accessory to the crime of the police.

Plaintiff has sued the John Doe Judge who issued the warrant; Honorable Eileen Koretz, Supervising Judge, Criminal Court of Manhattan; and Serena Springle, Borough Chief Clerk, Criminal Court of Manhattan. [U. S. District Court of the Southern District of New York (Complaint: #09 Civ. 1442 [HB])].

CPL 30 #160.10 (1.b) requires that fingerprints be obtained from a person accused of a misdemeanor. No fingerprints were obtained.

CPL 30 #30.10 (2.c) states that the prosecution of a misdemeanor must be commenced within two years. Since more than 27 months have passed since the alleged misdemeanors were committed, the time limit set by the statute of limitations has passed.

In summary 4 violations of CPL 30 have been identified. There can be no criminal prosecution of Plaintiff. Furthermore #2007NY029913 that Mr. McCann received from the District Attorney's office is the number on the unexecuted arraignment form. There is no case number for a criminal case, because no criminal case exists.

The criminal charges were formally dismissed by the Criminal court of Manhattan in the interest in justice on June 8, 2010, as a result of the events in the following chapter.

XIX. DISMISSAL OF THE CRIMINAL CASE

FIJA Demonstration of May 25, 2010

I arrived at the U. S. District Court at 500 Pearl Street in Manhattan, NY at 11:40 am on Tuesday, May 25, 2010. It was a warm and sunny day. Immediately a Homeland Security officer approached me and told me to leave. He was joined by officer Valentin, who told the first officer that I would be arrested. I continued to pass out the American Jury Institute pamphlet entitled "A Primer for Prospective Jurors" along with my handout which reads:

THE JUDGE WILL INSTRUCT THE JURY THAT IT MUST UPHOLD THE LAW AS HE GIVES IT.

HE WILL BE LYING.

THE JURY MUST JUDGE THE LAW AS WELL AS THE FACTS.

JURIES WERE INSTITUTED TO PROTECT THE CITIZENS FROM THE TYRANNY OF THEIR GOVERNMENT.

IT IS NOT THE DUTY OF THE JURY TO UPHOLD THE LAW.

IT IS THE JURY'S DUTY IS TO SEE THAT JUSTICE IS DONE.

At 12:00 noon Officer Barnes and a sergeant approached. Officer Barnes asked me to put down my sign, so that I would not hit him on the head with it. I declined saying that: "I am not going to hit you. It is not my style." Officer Barnes stood 5 feet in front of me and glowered. The sergeant stood 5 feet behind me.

I passed out literature, and Officer Barnes kept staring at me. I said to Barnes, "Nice day isn't it." He replied "Don't try to be friendly with me. I am not your friend." I apologized for offending him.

At 12:25 pm, I moved about 20 feet into the shade so that I could see the face of my cell phone better. Barnes yelled that I could not move there, but I ignored him. He placed me under arrest. Immediately I fell to the ground, as I always do when placed under arrest.

I was handcuffed behind my back. He had my arrest warrant from 3 years ago. He searched my clothes and took everything in my pockets. He said that the citation and a receipt for the confiscated property was in my tote bag. Another federal marshal said that if my fines were not paid within 10 days, he would issue another arrest warrant.

I was carried into the U. S. Courthouse and searched again. Then I was dragged to the isolation cell, which had only a bench and toilet. I urinated. The handcuffs were removed. A number of capillaries had been broken in my wrists. My hands had turned blue.

A short time later, I was handcuffed again and dragged down to a NY City police car. I was taken to the police holding cells in the aptly named Criminal Court of Manhattan building.

NY City Police Custody 5/25/10

At the police station my picture and thumb prints were taken. My belt and shoelaces were removed and kept by the police. The police could not decide if I should go before a magistrate or be sent to Bellevue Hospital psychiatric ward.

I was dragged upstairs to the courtroom and downstairs to the street level for transfer to Bellevue several times as they kept changing their minds. As a result, I was physically and verbally abused during these drags. My upper arms were crushed in their hands, and blood vessels broken. This was painful. My upper arms turned blue. My sneakers had no shoelaces, so my toes kept smashing into the front of the sneakers breaking blood vessels in my toes.

This was unpleasant to say the least. My toes turned blue, and did not return to normal for two weeks. While being dragged, my sweater, pants, and one sock fell off and were discarded in the hallways. I was given a sheer blue outfit of a top and pants to wear. The left pant leg was ripped to above the knee.

Finally I was taken before a magistrate. He was not identified, a custom of a court of inquisition. I was still handcuffed. I placed my head on the bench and never spoke to the magistrate. The magistrate gave a brief summary of events. He stated that I claimed that my commitment papers were not signed, which was true, so that I had never been committed. He said that the court copy was signed, thus admitting tampering of a legal document by the court.

The judge assigned a legal aid lawyer to talk with me outside the courtroom. I did not discuss the case with her, because I suspected that the courthouse was "bugged." When she returned she told the judge that I was polite, intelligent, and articulate, but would not discuss my case, because I claimed the courthouse was "bugged."

The magistrate replied that he could not tell if I was mentally competent. Obviously anyone who exercises his Fifth Amendment right to remain silent must be crazy. He ordered that I be sent to Bellevue Hospital psychiatric ward for evaluation. The hearing was recessed until June 8, 2010. I was dragged down the stairs in handcuffs, put in a police car, handcuffed to the back door, and delivered to Bellevue Hospital emergency admission.

Bellevue Hospital 5/25–5/26

In Bellevue, I was handcuffed to the bed. I was given a pair of hospital socks. I continued remaining silent. The nurses and doctors pounded on my chest and pinched my fingers, which was quite painful, but I would not utter a sound. Then they sodomized me by shoving a needle up my rectum. Presumably they were looking for drugs (or bombs).

Finally Dr. Goldberg, who was in charge of the emergency room, came and pleaded with me to talk to him. I stated that I was exercising my Fifth Amendment right to remain silent, and that I would talk to no-one while under arrest. These were the first words that I spoke to anyone since I was placed under arrest at the U. S. District Courthouse.

Exercising my Fifth Amendment right to remain silent was clear proof that I was insane. Dr. Goldberg stopped the medical exam and ordered that I be taken to the psychiatric ward. I was placed on a gurney and wheeled away to the psychiatric ward. I was placed in the sleep deprivation cell and the handcuffs removed. This room is a 20 by 6 feet room, 10 feet high. Except for the iron bar entrance gate, it had concrete block walls with no window, toilet, or sink. The only item in the room was a stuffed chair fixed directly below a bank of fluorescent lights. Since there was no toilet, I urinated on the floor.

After several hours, a doctor and four strong male attendants entered the room. The doctor said that he would give me a shot to put me to sleep and take x-rays. I objected vociferously, but the attendants pinned me to the floor while the doctor gave me an injection in my buttocks. Presumably this was a thorazine shot.

I passed out. The next thing I knew was that I woke up in another cell, and it was morning. I was lying on a wall bench. I was not informed nor have any idea what was done to my body while I was asleep. The cell had a toilet and sink.

I was let out of the cell and entered the common room in the psychiatric ward. I was given breakfast. This was the first food, liquid, or water that I had since leaving home at 9:00 am on the previous day. Then I played an interesting and somewhat wild game of chess with the grandson of Rocky Graziano. We were equally matched, so it was an interesting game.

While this was going on, a Mr. Miguel from Bellevue Hospital called my wife and asked if I had any psychiatric problems. My faithful wife lied and said that I was not crazy. She also failed to mention that I was a carrier of insanity. That was the psychiatric exam. I never saw a psychiatrist. It also was the first notice my wife had that I was arrested.

Then I and several others were handcuffed chain gang style to two other inmates, one to my right hand and one to my left hand in groups of about 6 people. We were taken in a paddy wagon back to the police station. I was dragged around some more.

Again, I was taken in a chain gang to a paddy wagon, and we were off to the Riker's Island prison. I still had not been given a receipt for any of my property. The paddy wagon consisted of several steel cages. The largest housed about 20 inmates. The smaller ones had one or two seats. I was alone in a two-seater still handcuffed. The leg room was less than in an economy seat in an airplane.

Apparently the smaller cells were for the more dangerous prisoners. Since I was incarcerated for holding signs on a public sidewalk at a demonstration across the street from the United Nations building, I was considered very dangerous. Probably I was considered to be engaging in treason, or at least espionage.

During the ride to Riker's Island the radio played very loud chain gang music. I guess that this was to drown out any talk of a breakout.

XX. RIKER'S ISLAND PRISON

Riker's Island Receiving 5/26–5/28

We arrived at Riker's Island Prison Receiving late Wednesday, May 26, 2010, not handcuffed, and 29 of us placed in a holding pen. It was a cement block cell with an iron gate and two windows, which barely opened. It was 20 feet by 15 feet by 10 feet high. It contained one bench 8 feet long by 8 inches wide. There was a toilet and a sink. The toilet had overflowed, so there was urine and feces on the floor. The sink could not be used for washing hands, because it was used as a garbage pail, since no garbage pail was present.

Sleeping was done by lying on the floor or sitting with your back on a wall. I got very little sleep in these pens, because I did not have room to lie down and my old body would ache in the sitting position. I had no dinner on Wednesday night. We were given individual identity badges. I was known to everyone as "Pops." This name stuck throughout my incarceration.

Soon we were moved to another holding pen which was larger: 20 x 20 x10 feet high. There were 40 of us in this pen. The toilet did not flush, so feces and urine accumulated in the toilet. After a while we were given a towel to place over the toilet to reduce the stench.

We were moved around from 3 holding pens, one 20 x 15 x 10 feet and two 20 x 20 x 10 feet. Apparently this was done, so that the pen that was empty could be cleaned. In the third pen, the toilet flushed, but there was still no useable water for washing hands. None of the pens had soap, towels or toilet paper. When the sinks became full of garbage, additional garbage was thrown on the floor.

During my stay, I met about 150 inmates, of whom 6 were Caucasian. The others were black or Latinos. The food was inedible. I had no dinner on Tuesday or Wednesday night.

Thursday night there was chicken, which was OK and inedible vegetables. Friday night dinner was two cold fish between two whole wheat bread slices plus some vegetables.

At Receiving, there was no telephone for inmates. None of us were allowed to make a telephone call. At one time we had 60 people in the pen occupying 400 square feet of floor space.

On Wednesday, May 26, or Thursday, May 27, (I forgot which night) at about 6:00 pm Rabbi Herbert Richtman, the Jewish chaplain visited me. The 5-minute interview was public and conducted through the prison bars. He checked to see if I was all right and notified my wife.

In the Receiving pens, marijuana was smoked openly. A few inmates would sit on the floor and roll joints. The guards knew this was taking place, but did not care. One inmate told me that the guards also smoke pot also while on duty, though I never witnessed this.

One day, the word was passed in the pen that the Cripps gang had been arrested and was in the adjoining pen. Soon word was passed that the turtles had arrive. The turtles were the riot squad, who wore face shields and body protective gear. They looked like turtles. They went into the pen with the Cripps. I could see nothing, but heard yelling and screaming. Then the turtles left.

Twice during my stay, I was taken to the medical area for evaluation by medical personnel. I told them that I had some old man problems and needed four prescription medicines and an aspirin every day. I was never given any medicine while in Receiving. There were two mens' bathrooms in medical, but neither had running water, soap, toilet paper, or towels. Inmates could not wash their hands in a medical area.

On one of my visits to medical, while waiting in the reception area, another inmate had a grand mal seizure, fell to the floor, and was rolling around. The other inmates screamed for help. It took about 10 minutes before two staff people showed up with a board. They rolled the inmate onto the board and strapped him to it. They lifted him to a gurney, wheeled him into the hall outside the reception area and left him there. No medical person attended to him, though they were within 30 feet of him.

On my second visit to medical, the nurse asked if I would rather go to general population or the hospital. I asked what the difference was. She told me that in the hospital, I would get a bed, so I chose the hospital. It turned out that there were beds in general population, but there were more inmates than beds.

On Friday, I again missed my supper, because I was handcuffed and driven to the NCI annex (the hospital). When we got there at 6:10 pm, I was refused entrance. We returned to the Receiving area. Much later that evening, I again was taken in handcuffs to the hospital and was admitted at 1:20 am early Saturday morning, May 29, 2010.

While I was in the Receiving area, my identification badge was taken from me. When we left for the hospital, I asked for it, but my request was refused. I arrived at the Hospital (NCI annex dorm 2B) without it, but was admitted. Without an ID badge, one does not exist and cannot receive medicine or go to any activity. Fortunately, I still had my wristlet ID from Bellevue, and that was accepted for purposes of medicine, law library, and outside recreation (one hour per day).

The linguistic skills of the NY City Police and the Receiving guards at Riker's Island are somewhat limited. They only use two words when they talk. One of these is" fuck," which is used both as a noun and verb. The other word is "fucking," which is used as an adjective. However the NY City police officer who had to drag me up and down stairs in the courthouse was more articulate. Every few minutes, he would say: "You worthless piece of shit," apparently directed at me.

Riker's Island NCI Hospital 5/28–6/8 (Psychiatric interview).

At the dorm room in the hospital, there were 27 inmates including me, 26 hospital beds with springs under the mattresses, and one cot with a metal slab under the mattress. I got the cot. The hospital population in that room varied from 24–27 while I was there.

I was given 2 sheets, a pillow case, a blanket, a towel, tee shirts, undershorts, an inmate handbook, an inmate rule book, and a large box for personal belongings. The linen and clothes were changed once a week. In between, we washed our own laundry. I did not have any pants, so an inmate loaned me a pair of his. My sneakers were removed and kept in property control. I was given a receipt for the sneakers and a pair of disposable orange slippers, called Patakis. Except for the sneakers, I was never given a receipt for any of my confiscated property.

There were two telephones in the dorm. We were allowed some free calls and some paid calls each day. I made my first call on Saturday evening, May 29, 2010, to my wife. These calls were collect long distance calls, because I live in New Jersey. Thus I did not get to make a telephone call until 4 days after my arrest.

Meals were at 4:30 am, 10:30 am, and 4:30 pm each day. The food was plentiful, wholesome, nutritious, and tasteless. Since this was a hospital, there were no condiments including salt or pepper. I was told that the food in general population was tastier. However the fruit, particularly the oranges and canned peaches, were excellent.

Lights out occurred at midnight. They went on again at 4:30 am for breakfast. After breakfast, there was a two hour lights out period. The breakfast room had a TV, which was controlled by the alpha male.

Medicine was distributed 4 times a day. I got mine at 10:00 am and 9:00 pm. Also my blood pressure and temperature were taken 3 times a day. The medicines that I received daily were my 4 prescription medicines and an aspirin, but that did not start until Tuesday, June 1, 2010.

The other inmates were helpful to me and each other. Everyone seemed to get along. The hospital was run well.

The male guards were pleasant and helpful. Some of the female guards were bitches, but they were just trying to let us know who was boss. The only real problem was getting anything fast. It took me seven days before I was getting all of my medicines. My wife sent me two packages. The first was given to me the day after it arrived at the prison. The second contained my legal material, was refused by the prison, and returned to my home. In addition I received a letter from someone that I did not know who offered his help in the fully informed jury activities.

I called my wife almost every day at about 6:00 pm starting on Sunday, May 30, 2010. Soon after I arrived, it was learned that I tried my own legal cases and had tried about 50 cases. Everyone came to me for advice and help in preparing grievances and legal papers. I became a jailhouse lawyer.

There was a Gideon bible in the dorm. I read the whole book of all 150 psalms. The other inmates noticed this and made me their spiritual adviser. Also there was book lying around ("Life Expectancy" by Dean Koontz) which I read, and it was hilarious. As a result, I woke up one morning to find that every book in the place was under my bed. Now I was the dorm librarian. This did not occupy much time, since few of the inmates read anything or, in many cases, were able to read at all. For those that could read, they were limited to words of less than 4 syllables. When these long words came along they came to me to pronounce them and tell them what they meant. Thus I became a reading counselor.

I also went into the pants pressing business. Since mine was the only bed with a flat metal slab to support the mattress, the inmates would lay their pants on the slab and then return the mattress on top of the pants. While I was sleeping at night, I was pressing pants.

I also provided some entertainment for the prisoners. I have a large number of jokes that I like to tell. Unfortunately, most people will not listen. However here I had a captive audience with essentially nothing else to do, so I regaled them with my sick humor. During my stay in prison everyone referred to me as, and called me, "Pops."

The TV was controlled by the alpha male. Lots of sports events and trash TV shows, mostly of young girls who had sex with six guys and did not know which one was the father of their fetus.

Early in my visit blood samples were drawn for testing to check if my medicines could be given to me. My blood pressure varied from 132/85 to 98/62 and temperature from 96.1 to 98.4 during my stay. The daily routine consisted of:

4:30 am: lights on and breakfast
6:00–8:00 am lights out
Medical calls 7:00 am, 10:00 am, 1:00 pm 3:00 pm, 5:00 pm, and 9:30 pm
Individual medical calls throughout the day
10:30 lunch
1:00 recreation for 1 hour in the yard
5:00 law library for 2 hours
Blood pressure and temperature 3 times per day.
Bed count 2 times a day.

Next to my bed on one side was an inmate named Saint Julian Mack. He is a mixed breed of several Native American tribes. He was extremely helpful and kind to me. He saw that I received proper care.

On Sunday, May 30, 2010, at 10:30 am, I had my first bowel movement since I left my home at 9:00 am on Tuesday, May 25. I took a shower, put on fresh prison clothes and borrowed pants from an inmate. I discarded my blue tissue prison garments.

I also was the communications person. I let several of the inmates use my allotted telephone calls, since I did not need them, because I had to call my wife collect.

Sunday, 5–30–10

On Sunday at 6:00 am some guy got a razor and cut up my face pretty severely. That guy was me. It was my first shave since I left home the previous Tuesday morning. There was no shaving cream or after shave lotion. One soaped his face and started cutting. The wall mirrors were defective and essentially worthless.

Initially I had no pillow. I used my towel as a pillow. Later I got another blanket and put that inside my pillowcase to make a pillow.

Tuesday, 6–1–10

On Tuesday, 6–1–10, I received a thorough medical exam. After lunch I went to the yard, chain ganged to 3 other inmates. We were handcuffed to another inmate by one hand, leaving one hand free. Then the 2 pairs were chained together one pair in front and one behind.We were unchained in the yard. There were 17 of us in the yard. Four officers were outside eating lunch.

The yard was a 42 x 60 feet asphalt surface open to the sky. The fences were 12 feet high topped by 5 more feet of barbed wire. There was a basketball backboard and basket. Four of us, including me, shot buckets for awhile. Then I rested. It was warm and sunny day. Five inmates were working out with weights. One inmate was practicing a dance routine. A few inmates just sat and soaked up the sun. After an hour we were chained together again and returned to the hospital dorm. I was interviewed by Benjamin Campbell, a psychiatrist.

Wednesday 6–2–10

On Wednesday, 6–2–10, I was told that I had a visitor and to collect my stuff. I returned the pants that I had borrowed and proceeded to leave in my under shorts. A guard found a pair of brown pants. There were two large rips in the pants.

Joe McNichols, a retired firefighter from Queens, visited me for 1 hour. I had never met Joe, but we have had some e-mail correspondence. We told jokes and had a good time. Even the guards laughed, probably a violation of discipline.

Joe smuggled in a pocket constitution so that I could start sedition. After he left, he called my wife, which she greatly appreciated. I was strip searched, handcuffed, and returned to the dorm.

The other inmates started teaching me ghetto talk. I learned two phrases: "Whas up homey" (homey means homeboy, which is a bit of a putdown.) "Ho down, Pimp up." What this is supposed to mean, I do not know, but I suspect it is sexist in some manner. It is also not clear when to use this phrase with my orthodox Jewish neighbor matrons.

Thursday 6–3–10

I had a blood test for HIV, and found out that I was leading a dull life, since I tested negative. I filled out a grievance form for another inmate. I noticed that the one guard in our dorm was sound asleep and apparently in a catatonic state. The inmates could have chopped him up easily, and he would never have recovered. Apparently he forgot the primary rule for guards to be always alert for trouble.

At midnight I was notified that I was going to court tomorrow. Be ready to leave at 6:00 am.

The law library had many legal books. It also had three computers which only had access to Lexus Nexus, the online legal library. There also was a copying machine in the library.

Friday, 6–4–10

On Friday, June 4, 2010, I left the dorm at 6:10 am and walked to a holding pen, where I stripped to my underpants, blue socks, and orange Patakis. I was given a tee shirt and a pair of brown pants with two large rips. Over them, I donned an orange jump suit.

At 8:30 am, I tried to talk to a guard, but he ignored me. At 8:45 am the other cellmates were removed, and I was alone in the cell. Then other inmates joined me. The cell was cleaned at 9:45 am.

At 10:00, I was loaded into a bus with cages. It had a 20 seat cage section, and five 1 or 2 seaters with less leg room than an economy airplane seat. I was alone, handcuffed in a 2 seater.

At 11:20, we reached the aptly named Criminal Courthouse of Manhattan. I was put in a cage with 5 other guys. The handcuffs were removed. The cage was 20' x 20' x 10' high. It had a toilet and sink, but no running water. There were no towels or toilet paper. At 11:30, I was taken uncuffed to another holding cell where I got a peanut butter and jelly sandwich and tea.

At 12:30, I was taken to a room with a psychiatrist and his assistant. They did not introduce themselves. The assistant asked the questions, and the psychiatrist wrote the answers. They interviewed me from 12:30 to 1:30 pm. At the end of the interview I asked for their names, but they did not give them. They said that they would be on the written report.

They asked trick questions like "Are steam and ice different substances?" Since I am a professor of chemistry, I got that one. I used the same question on some exams that I gave. They also asked me to count down by sevens from 100 (answer: 100, 93, 86,

79, etc). They also wanted to know what my legal defense would be, so they could tell the judge. I refused to answer that question.

They wanted to know if I would post bail. I said absolutely not. They asked even if it was $1.00. I said that I would not even post $1.00 as a matter of principle. They asked if I knew what my maximum sentence could be. I responded 1 year, but that would be an unusually severe sentence.

They asked if I had or needed a lawyer. I responded that I do not do business with the criminal class, and that a lawyer does not represent the interests of his client, but is an officer of the court. I gave my speech about the corruption of lawyers and elected legislators. I said that I would represent myself since I could do and say things in court that a lawyer never would (unless he wanted to be disbarred).

They asked why am I doing the actions that get me arrested. I responded because we live in a totalitarian country with a judicial system like those of Hitler and Stalin and the largest prison population in the world. I wanted my children and grandchildren to live in a free country, but it probably is too late for my children. I cried.

After the interview, I was returned to the holding cell with a toilet and sink, but no running water, toilet paper, or towels. At 3:50 pm, I was moved to another cell. While on the elevators, the inmates, who are handcuffed, are required to look at the back of the elevator. At 4:30, I was given milk and a cheese sandwich.

At 7:00 pm, I was handcuffed in front, taken out of the cell. Nine of us were put into the van with cells and returned to Riker's Island. I was in a single seater, still handcuffed. We arrived back at Riker's Island prison at 8:10 pm. I was given my medicines, and my blood pressure was taken. My bedding was gone, so I slept in my cot with one blanket, but no linen.

Saturday, 6–5–10

I received a letter from someone in Virginia who had heard of me, but whom I did not know, asking how he could help. I was touched by his concern.

I met a new inmate who was a 16 year old boy with his mouth wired shut. Imagine putting a 16 year old boy, who could not talk, in a room full of sex-starved, adult, male criminals!

That evening I filed a grievance stating that I had been in the medical dorm for 6 days and never received cocoa and graham crackers at bedtime. I put in a request for these items, but never received a reply. At the rate things happened there, I suppose they are still mulling over that grievance deciding what to do. Undoubtedly this was the first grievance of that nature that they had to deal with. At 10:05 pm, I called home and spoke with my wife, daughter, and 3-year old granddaughter.

Sunday, 6–6–10

On Sunday, June 6, 2010, lights and breakfast did not commence until 5:00 am. Apparently, Sunday is a day of rest. By now I had developed a bad cough which occurs when I get insufficient sleep. I had no top sheet and only one blanket, so I was cold continuously. My arm bruises were almost gone. The pain in my toenails was gone, but my toenails were still discolored.

Monday, 6–7–10

There was laundry change. I received two fresh bedsheets, a pillow case and a towel. At 12:30 pm, my identification badge was taken away, and I was moved from Dorm 2B, which was a low violence dorm, to Dorm 1, which was a no violence dorm and had 40 beds. I was given two buckets for keeping my belongings. Also I had a real hospital bed with a spring base. There were 4 other Caucasians; the other inmates were blacks and Latinos.

At 5:40 pm, I called my wife and explained that I was moved from a low violence dorm to a no violence dorm. While on the phone a loud shouting match broke out. Two prisoners were after each other. The guards moved in, ordered everyone to their beds, and broke up the scuffle. My wife heard all of this. I am sure she was comforted to know that now I was in a no violence dorm.

After the scuffle was calmed down, I entertained the inmates with my collection of jokes. It was nice to have a captive audience.

Tuesday, 6–8–10

At 4:45 am, I awoke, showered, shaved, dressed, and left for the Criminal Court of Manhattan at 5:50 am. I went through the same process as the previous Friday. This time I did not see a psychiatrist, but had a court appearance. I was the last inmate to have an appearance. At 5:20 pm, I was handcuffed and brought to the courtroom by a guard. The court had been emptied and closed. The only people present were a judge, a court reporter, a young lady from the district attorney's office, the guard, and me.

The young assistant district attorney announced that "In the case of the people of the State of New York versus Julian Heicklen, the state moves that the case be dismissed in the interest of justice." The handcuffs were removed and I was free to go.

I had no money and no way to go home. I was directed to the cashier's window. The cashier was away for dinner. When he returned at 6:30 pm, he gave me $16.32, which what was left of the $20.10 confiscated by Homeland Security on May 25, 2010.

Some of my money had been used by other inmates that I let make calls off of my account. I bought a metro card, took the subway to the Port Authority, caught a bus for Teaneck, NJ. I borrowed a bus rider's cell phone to call my wife, who met me at the bus stop.

Recovery of Property

On Tuesday, June 15, 2010, I went to Manhattan to recover my property. At 12:30 pm, I was at NY City Police headquarters at 1 Plaza Place where the property recovery center is situated. I was denied entry, because I did not have a case number or voucher. I was directed to go to 1 White Street, about 3 blocks away, to obtain these documents. When I arrived there, I was informed that I was at a jail that had nothing to do with property reclamation. I was sent across the street to property control.

There I was advised that only property in the possession of corrections, and not the police, could be recovered. I was instructed to call 311 to make an appointment to get my prison property at Riker's Island. Further I was told to return to police headquarters at 1 Plaza Place.

I returned to police headquarters, but refused entry again. I was directed to go to Room 732, Criminal Court of Manhattan at 100 Centre Street to get the appropriate documentation. When I got there, I was asked who made the arrest, and I told them the Department of Homeland Security. Then I was informed that I had to go to them to arrange to get my property.

Since I was in the Criminal Court of Manhattan, I decided to get copies of the court order dismissing the case, the psychiatric evaluation of June 4, 2010, and the $210.00 the court was "holding" (actually stealing) for me. I never did find out how to get the money. I went to the Clerk of Court's office, Room 150, and obtained a copy of the court order and the names of the presiding judges involved in my case. The Clerk had signed the court order. The judge's name did not appear on the Order, which seemed strange to me.

The Clerk sent me back to room 732 to get the voucher. When I got there, I was told that I would have to call Patrol Boro Manhattan South for the voucher. The Clerk also said to go to room 500 to get the psychiatric report. When I got there, the person said that I could not have it, because it was the court's property. (I was always under the impression that medical records could not be denied to the patient.) She said that she would not release it unless the judge issued a subpoena.

I returned to the Clerk of Court's office to get a subpoena form. He did not have them, but directed me to the Clerk of Court in the NY State Supreme Court at Room 109B, 60 Centre Street. When I got there, the Clerk told me to go to room 141B. While I was looking for room 141B, which is tucked in some alcove somewhere, I ran into a court official and asked him how to get there. He was puzzled by this request and asked me for what reason. When I told him, he said that I should go to room 116.

When I got to room 116, the clerk gave me several pages of instructions for filing a subpoena, but said that the court could not provide the subpoena forms, because they were copyrighted, and that I would have to buy one from a bookseller. He also suggested that instead, I just write a motion to the judge to order Room 500 to give me a copy of my medical record. However, when I told him that my case had been dismissed and was closed, he thought the judge could no longer issue any orders, but it was worth a try. To file a subpoena, I would have to open a new case with the court and pay a filing fee of $210.00.

It was now 5:00 pm, and the courts were closing for the day. I will try the court order route, but it is a long shot. I still have not had any property returned. I will have to contact Homeland Security for a voucher that I can present at 1 PLaza Place to get my property, if it is even there. I do not hold out much hope of getting a voucher from Homeland Security, because probably it will tell me that all of my property has been transferred to the NY City police, which I believe has happened. However, I was able to obtain the psychiatrist's report and the $210.00 from the Criminal Court Clerk.

THIS IS YOUR GOVERNMENT IN ACTION

Concluding Observations

I was never informed of my Fifth Amendment right to remain silent by the Homeland Security police, the federal marshals, the NY City police, any court officials, the legal defense lawyer, any Bellevue Hospital personal, Department of Corrections officials, the psychiatrist who interviewed me in the Criminal Court of Manhattan, or anyone else. On the contrary, I was verbally and physically abused for remaining silent. I should have been allowed to make a telephone call within 24 hours, but it was 3–1/3 days before I could make a call.

I did not receive my medicines until I was in the infirmary, 5 days after my arrest, except for one dose of milk of magnesia on Thursday, May 27, 2010. Even then I did not get my daily dose of Metamucil until several days later.

Except for the visit by Rabbi Herbert Richtman, the prison chaplain, through the bars of the receiving pen, I was not permitted to see a Jewish chaplain. There was a Catholic nun that came into the ward three times during my stay, and I talked with her each time. These were mostly social calls.

I also was not permitted to see social services or legal aid. I did go to the yard one day and to the legal library on two occasions. I was sent to Bellevue Hospital for a psychiatric exam, but had no exam and did not even see a psychiatrist.

Both Joe McNichols and bile (the nickname of my photographer) contacted my wife to keep her informed of my situation while I was away. This was of great solace to her. Thanks guys.

XXI. THE DVD VIDEO EVIDENCE

In my letter of August 6, 2009, I further wrote to Judge Koeltl:

"In his letter of July 31, 2009, Mr. McCann raised a new issue based on DVD video evidence of the incident of April 17, 2007. He argues that the video shows that there is irrefutable evidence that there is no material evidence for trial. On the other hand, I argue that the video provides irrefutable evidence of the guilt of the police officers. This is a dispute of fact, not of law."

"In order to resolve this contradiction requires the questioning of witnesses, a discussion of issues and interpretations by both sides (opening and closing statements at a trial), and a decision by a jury of peers. A judge is not permitted to decide issues of fact if a jury trial is demanded. A judge can decide if evidence is admissible. Since both Mr. McCann and I wish to have the DVD video entered as evidence, I do not see this as an issue."

"Furthermore I have listed all the facts of the incident commencing on April 17, 2007, in my complaint to the Court and the accompanying documents. It is my contention that these documents provide irrefutable evidence of the guilt of the police officers in denying my constitutional rights. If the Court wishes to have me affirm my statements under penalty of perjury as witnessed by a notary public or a person able to perform an oath, I will be happy to comply."

"Mr. McCann also argues that Police Commissioner Kelly should not be a defendant. This issue has already been discussed twice; once by Judge Wood and once by Judge Baer. Judge Baer allowed Commissioner Kelly to be included. How many times does this issue have to be resolved?"

"I hope that this letter will convince you that Mr. McCann's new issue concerning the DVD evidence must be decided at trial. If not, I will need considerable time to digest his information, especially since I will be in La Jolla, CA from August 8-16. In order to research all of the laws and decisions that Mr. McCann quotes will require about one month after my return."

"Frankly, I am losing my patience. Mr. McCann has no legitimate case and is just fishing for excuses and delays. His hope is that he can delay this trial until I die. I cite the following:"

> "1. He demanded my social security number in violation of law and for no apparent reason. It certainly could not help him get information from the state courts, because those courts do not have my social security number. He probably was going to use that number to investigate my private affairs in order to cast doubt on my character."
>
> "2. Mr. McCann convinced you to order me to provide information that I do not have and that I have demonstrated does not exist. He falsified his request to you by claiming that I would not provide release forms."
>
> "3. Three times I sent Interrogatories to Mr. McCann to provide identities of the John Doe Police officers. So far he has ignored two of these and has until August 15, 2009, to respond to the third. I filed a motion for you to order Mr. McCann to provide that information, but you denied my motion. I filed a second motion, but the Clerk of the District Court returned it with the statement that the Court does not help litigants with discovery."
>
> "4. On March 2, 2009, Defendants Toala and Kelly were served with a Summons, Amended Complaint, and Plaintiff interrogatories to discover identities and addresses of John Doe Defendants. Mr. McCann entered as counsel

for Defendant Toala on July 17, 2009, well after the 30-day limitation."

"5. At the hearing of July 17, 2009, Mr. McCann brought up the issue of a stay of the civil case until the criminal trial is over. Since there is no criminal trial and never was one, apparently he has now dropped this issue."

"6. His latest ploy is to ask for dismissal of the case based on the claim that the DVD video shows that there is irrefutable evidence that there is no material evidence for trial. Exactly the opposite is true. However the truth or falseness of that claim is irrelevant at this time. A jury must make that decision."

"7. He claims that Commissioner Kelly should not be a defendant, even though two judges (Wood and Baer) have already discussed this, and Judge Baer ruled that he could be."

"It is your duty as a judge to order Mr. McCann to stop this nonsense. If he does not, then he should be found in contempt of court."

On August 18, 2009, I again wrote to Judge Koeltl in response to Mr. McCann's motion to dismiss based on the DVD video.

A. IRREFUTABLE EVIDENCE

Mr. McCann claims that the video shows irrefutable evidence of my guilt. The American Heritage Dictionary of the English Language defines irrefutable as "impossible to refute or disprove; incontrovertible: irrefutable arguments; irrefutable evidence of guilt." I refute Mr. McCann's claim. Therefore the video is not irrefutable. This is a syllogism of Aristotle. It is a foundation of logical thinking. If you were a reasonable person, I could end this letter here, since my response is sufficient to discard Mr. McCann's claim. However I realize that logic has no standing in the law.

I am not the only person who disputes the McCann claim. The prosecuting Assistant District Attorney also believes that there was no evidence of my guilt. He offered to drop the charges and dismiss the case, if I promised not to get arrested in the next six months nor to sue the police. I refused this offer. He never convened a Grand Jury to indict me. He never entered an appearance with the Criminal Court of Manhattan. Likewise the Criminal Court of Manhattan did not think that there was sufficient evidence to hold a trial. No judge entered the case. The Court ignored all my inquiries. In particular the Court ignored my request for a *habeas corpus* hearing; my request for the purpose of the June 20, 2007, hearing; and for the request that the Court order the Assistant District Attorney to impanel a Grand Jury. I never received any written correspondence from the Criminal Court of Manhattan, except for the unsigned arraignment documents. Presumably, the Court issued a bench warrant for my arrest. However no attempt was made to enforce that order. It was purely cosmetic in order to protect the police in their criminal activities.

The nurse that came to my aid in the video did not believe that there was irrefutable evidence for my arrest, since she pleaded with the police not to arrest me.

Mr. McCann claims that the DVD video provides irrefutable evidence of my guilt. Nowhere in the video am I placed under arrest by the police. However the video does show the police dragging and carrying me away. I was incarcerated for a day. This constitutes kidnapping, or at least unlawful imprisonment.

B. DEFINITIONS OF KIDNAPPING

Kidnapping is defined as "The crime of unlawfully seizing and carrying away a person by force or fraud, or seizing and

detaining a person against his or her will with an intent to carry that person away at a later time."
(dictionary.thefreedictionary.com/Kidnapping)

New York State Law Article 135 states: S135.00 Unlawful imprisonment, kidnapping and custodial interference; definitions of terms. The following definitions are applicable to this article:

1. "Restrain" means to restrict a person`s movements intentionally and unlawfully in such manner as to interfere substantially with his liberty by moving him from one place to another, or by confining him either in the place where the restriction commences or in a place to which he has been moved, without consent and with knowledge that the restriction is unlawful. A person is so moved or confined "without consent" when such is accomplished by:

   (a) physical force, intimidation or deception
2. "Abduct" means to restrain a person with intent to prevent his liberation by either

   (a) secreting or holding him in a place where he is not likely to be found. (I point out that my daughter could not find me until contacted later by the police.)

   S 135.05 Unlawful imprisonment in the second degree. A person is guilty of unlawful imprisonment in the second degree when he restrains another person. Unlawful imprisonment in the second degree is a class A misdemeanor.

   S135.25 §2(d). Kidnapping in the first degree. A person is guilty of kidnapping in the first degree when he abducts another person and when:
3. He restrains the person abducted for a period of more than twelve hours with intent to

   (d) Interfere with the performance of a governmental or political function;

C. SPECIFIC RESPONSES TO MEMORANDUM OF LAW

Local Civil Rule 56.1 (a) states:

> "Upon any motion for summary judgment pursuant to Rule 56 of the Federal Rules of Civil Procedure, there shall be annexed to the notice of motion a separate, short and concise statement, in numbered paragraphs, of the material facts as to which the moving party contends there is no genuine issue to be tried. Failure to submit such a statement may constitute grounds for denial of the motion."

Since Mr. McCann failed to follow this rule, this is grounds for denial of the motion. However I have responded by referring to page numbers of his supporting document, instead of numbered paragraphs as requested in Local Civil Rule 56.1 (b).

On page 3, Mr. McCann states: "which plaintiff estimates was 35 feet behind the stairs were (sic) the rabbis had been seated." This and other distances reported by me were not estimates. Two days after the incident, (on April 19, 2007), I returned to the scene and measured all distances with a tape measure. In each case the distances reported were about 4 inches less than the actual distances measured, since I rounded down to the nearest foot, because that was the limit of accuracy.

On page 6, Mr. McCann argues that Commissioner Kelly was not personally involved in the arrest. I do not agree with that statement. My contention is that Commissioner Kelly was personally responsible for breaking up the demonstration. Several police officers were involved, so that this was not the random indiscretion of one or a few police officers.

This demonstration had been well publicized many days before it occurred. Dozens of police officers had accompanied us from the Iranian embassy to the Isaiah Wall. Police Commissioner Kelly was well aware of this demonstration, and the police were acting under his orders, or at least under department policy. This issue was considered by Judge Baer, and he agreed to permit Commissioner Kelly to be a Defendant.

On page 8, the deposition states: "Probable cause exists when, based on the totality of circumstances, the officer has knowledge of, or reasonably trustworthy information as to, facts and circumstances that are sufficient to warrant a person of reasonable caution in the belief that an offense has been, or is being committed by the person to be arrested." I had read Amendment I of the U. S. Constitution to the police officers, so that they were well aware that they were violating my constitutional rights. Furthermore they committed crimes by ordering me into a crowd (reckless endangerment) which was blocking pedestrian traffic.

On page 9, it is stated that a person is guilty of disorderly conduct when he "congregates with other persons in a public place and refuses to comply with a lawful order of the police to disperse." The police did not issue a lawful order. In fact the police did not order me to disperse. They ordered me to congregate.

The DVD video shows that I was not disrupting vehicular or pedestrian traffic, as alleged on page 9.

On page 10, the claim is made that I refused to obey 5 orders to disperse. I was never given an order to disperse. I was ordered to congregate. It would have been impossible to disperse, since I was standing alone.

Nowhere in the video was it shown that I was placed under arrest. The Memorandum of Law is a tissue of lies. Mr. McCann should be arrested and tried for perjury. At least, Mr. McCann should be found in Contempt of Court. In addition, I inform you that the police have tampered with the DVD video. Some of the sound track has been erased.

D. LIMITATIONS OF JUDGES' PREROGATIVES

I remind you that I have requested a jury trial, so that it is not the prerogative of a judge to decide the facts. That is the duty of the jury. In support of this statement I quote several U. S. Court decisions. These are:

In Morissette v United States, 342 U. S. 246 (1952), the U. S. Supreme Court recognized the powers of juries to engage in nullification. The court stated: "Had the jury convicted on proper instructions it would be the end of the matter. But juries are not bound by what seems inescapable logic to judges....They might have refused to brand Morissette as a thief. Had they done so, that too would have been the end of the matter."

Likewise, the U. S. Supreme Court in Duncan v. Louisiana, 391 U. S. 145 (1968), implicitly endorsed the policies behind nullification when it stated: "If the defendant preferred the common-sense judgment of the jury to the more tutored but less sympathetic reaction of the single judge, he was to have it."

U. S. Supreme Court Justice Byron White [Duncan v. Louisiana 391 U. S. 145, 156 (1968)] said: "The purpose of a jury is to guard against the exercise of arbitrary power, to make available the commonsense judgment of the community as a hedge against the overzealous or mistaken prosecutor and in preference to the professional or perhaps overconditioned or biased response of a judge."

In a 1972 decision (U. S. v Dougherty, 473 F 2nd 1113, 1139), the Court said: "The pages of history shine on instances of the jury's exercise of its prerogative to disregard instructions of the judge."

E. LOCAL CIVIL RULE 56

In accordance with Local Civil Rule 56 (e) (2), I affirm, under penalty of perjury, that all information provided in this letter is true and accurate to the best of my knowledge.

In accordance with Local Civil Rule 56 (g), I contend that the affidavit was submitted in bad faith, solely for the purpose of delay, and that it contains errors of fact known to Mr. McCann. The rule further states that "the court must order the submitting party to pay the reasonable expenses, including attorney fees, that it incurred as a result. An offending party or attorney may also be held in contempt."

I demand that Mr. McCann be found in contempt. I consider this letter to end the request of Mr. McCann to dismiss this case based on the evidence of the DVD video.

XXII. MOTION FOR CONTEMPT

On August 28, 2008, I wrote to Judge Koeltl asking for contempt proceedings against the Defendants. Enclosed were a notarized affidavit, **NOTICE OF MOTIONS**, and a **MEMORANDUM OF LAW IN SUPPORT OF CONTEMPT PROCEEDINGS AGAINST COUNSELS FOR DEFENSE MICHAEL A. CARDOZO AND MAX MCCANN**. An Affidavit and Certificate of Service are included in the memorandum.

I mentioned that the current pace of this trial is unacceptable. Remedies are suggested in the enclosed memorandum. If the submitted motions are not ordered and executed by September 15, 2009, I will consider Max McCann, Michael Cardozo, and you to be in collusion for the purpose of obstructing justice. Appropriate remedies will be pursued.

A courtesy copy of this material is being sent to the *Pro Se* Clerk. Please instruct that office to retain this material and include it in the case record. If this conflicts with a Court rule, ignore the rule.

In the Contempt Memorandum I included the following:

C. CLAIMS

I. Late entry of Defendant Toala

Defendants Toala and Kelly were served on March 2, 2009. On July 17, 2009, Attorneys McCann and Cardozo made an entry for Defendant Toala, 3-1/2 months after it was due. The summons served on Defendants Toala and Kelly reads, in part:

> "**SUMMONS IN A CIVIL ACTION** To: (Defendant's name and address) A lawsuit has been filed against you. Within 20 days after service of this summons on you (not

counting the day you received it) or 60 days if you are the United States or a United States agency, or an officer or employee of the United States described in Fed. R. Civ. P. 12 (a)(2) or (3) you must serve on the plaintiff an answer to the attached complaint or a motion under Rule 12 of the Federal Rules of Civil Procedure. The answer or motion must be served on the plaintiff or plaintiff's attorney, whose name and address are: If you fail to respond, judgment by default will be entered against you for the relief demanded in the complaint. You also must file your answer or motion with the court."

Notice that the last statement says the judgment by default will (not may) be entered against you. The only exceptions are given in Federal rules of Civil Procedure (FRCP) Rule 6 (1) which states:

(1) In General.

When an act may or must be done within a specified time, the court may, for good cause, extend the time: (A) with or without motion or notice if the court acts, or if a request is made, before the original time or its extension expires; or

(B) on motion made after the time has expired if the party failed to act because of excusable neglect.

Neither of these exceptions are applicable here. Therefore the Court must render judgment against Defendant Toala.

II. Harassment of Plaintiff

Attorney McCann and his paralegal, Nicole Wright, harassed Plaintiff by sending numerous letters requesting the execution of the release forms. (March 19, 2009; April 2, 2009; May 8, 2009; May 13, 2009; June 12, 2009, letter to Judge Koeltl).

Plaintiff sent these forms twice to Mr. McCann; once on April 6, 2009; and once on April 20, 2009. Two of their letters were sent prior to Plaintiff's first submission; and 3, after the second submission. In their letters they always refer to Plaintiff's claim of the incident of April 17, 2007, as a claim of "false arrest." This is a euphemism used by the legal profession to obfuscate the event it describes. It is an oxymoron. There is no such thing as a false arrest. Plaintiff refers to the incident of April 17, 2007, to be a "kidnapping ."

Mr. McCann has made repeated telephone calls to Plaintiff badgering him for the release forms, even after he submitted them. Plaintiff found these calls sufficiently annoying, that finally he refused to accept them.

III. Illegal request of Plaintiff's social security number

In his letters, Mr. McCann made illegal requests for Plaintiff's social security number. He had no legitimate need for this information, since none of the New York State courts had this number. The United States Social Security Administration policy states: (http://www.ssa.gov/pubs/10002.html#protect)

> "We maintain the privacy of Social Security records unless:
> The law requires us to disclose information to another government agency; or
> Your information is needed to conduct Social Security or other government health or welfare program business."
>
> "You should be very careful about sharing your number and card to protect against misuse of your number. Giving your number is voluntary even when you are asked for the number directly. If requested, you should ask: Why your number is needed; How your number will be used;
>
> What happens if you refuse; and What law requires you to give your number. The answers to these questions can help you decide if you want to give your Social Security number. The decision is yours."

IV. Refusal to respond to interrogatories

Discovery disclosure is required as stated in Rule 26(a)(1)(A):

> "Rule 26. Duty to Disclose; General Provisions Governing Discovery
> (a) Required Disclosures. (1) Initial Disclosures. (A) In General. Except as exempted by Rule 26(a) (1)(B) or as otherwise stipulated or ordered by the court, a party must, without awaiting a discovery request, provide to the other parties:
> (i) the name and, if known, the address and telephone number of each individual likely to have discoverable information "along with the subjects of that information" that the disclosing party may use to support its claims or defenses, unless the use would be solely for impeachment;"

Three times Plaintiff submitted Interrogatories to Attorney McCann to produce discovery material.(February 28, 2009; April 6, 2009, and July 27, 2009); Each interrogatory has been ignored.

After each Interrogatory was submitted, Plaintiff submitted motions to order Defendants to respond to the interrogatories. (February 28, 2009; April 6, 2009; and August 28, 2009).

The first motion was denied by Judge Koeltl on the flimsy reason that not enough information was available. Did Judge Koeltl really believe that Defendant Toala did not know which police officers assisted him in the kidnapping?

The second motion was returned to Plaintiff by the Clerk of Court with the statement that the Court does not aid in discovery.

No action has been taken by the Court on the third motion, which accompanies this Memorandum.

V. Providing misinformation about the facts

In his letter of May 8, 2009, to Judge Koeltl, Mr. McCann stated incorrectly that Plaintiff had not submitted release forms. As a result, Judge Koeltl was tricked into ordering Plaintiff on May 12, 2009, to provide information that he did not have, and which does not exist. This made Judge Koeltl an accessory to the obstruction of justice. In his letter of June 12, 2009, Mr. McCann falsely states that Plaintiff: "has not provided the executed consent and authorization for release of records."

In his letter of July 1, 2009, Mr. McCann stated that the "criminal charges stemming from plaintiff's arrest on or about April 17, 2007, ...are currently pending in New York County Criminal Court." He further states that the case number of the criminal case is 2007NY029913. At the conference of July 17, 2009, Counsel Elizabeth Daitz repeated this statement.

Both statements are false. The number 2007NY029913 is the docket number of the unexecuted arraignment form. There is no criminal case number, because there is no criminal case. In her letter of May 13, 2009, Nicole Wright states that Plaintiff claims that his criminal case was dismissed. Plaintiff never made such a claim, because he asserts that there never was a criminal case.

VI. Introducing tampered evidence

On July 20, 2009, Mr. McCann submitted a tampered video as evidence. The most important part of the sound track, in which Plaintiff is placed "under arrest," is missing.

VII. Stalling to delay proceedings in order to obstruct justice

Defendants are acting in bad faith. They are attempting to stall the proceedings until the Plaintiff dies. They were served on March 2, 2009, so their response was due on April 4, 2009. However, Judge Koeltl extended the time to respond to April 15, 2009. On April 12, 2009, he further extended the response time to

May 15, 2009. On May 15, 2009, Judge Koeltl again extended Defendant's time to June 26, 2009; on July 17, 2009, until July 31, 2009; on July 20, 2009, until August 23, 2009; on August 14, 2009, until September 18, 2009.

On June 12, 2009, Counsel Max McCann requested that "Plaintiff 's Complaint be dismissed pursuant to Fed R. Civ. P 16 (f), 41(b) and 37(b)(2) (C) for Plaintiff 's failure to prosecute this matter and failed to comply with Court Orders."

On July 17, 2009, at the conference, Attorney Daitz requested that the Judge issue a stay until the criminal case was resolved. Plaintiff responded that a stay would amount to burying the case, since there is no criminal case.

On July 17, 2009, Attorneys McCann and Cardozo made an entry for Defendant Toala, 3-1/2 months after it was due.

On July 31, 2009, Attorneys McCann and Cardozo submitted Motions and a Memorandum of Law to dismiss the civil case. This was based on evidence in the DVD video. The arguments presented were ridiculous on their face. In any event, a judge cannot dismiss a case in a jury trial based on a judgment of the facts or evidence.

VIII. Summary

In summary, Plaintiff accuses Defendants of the following:

a. belated entry of Defendant Toala
b. harassment of Plaintiff
c. illegally requesting Plaintiff 's social security number
d. entrapment of Judge Koeltl into being a coconspirator to obstruct justice
e. refusal to respond to interrogatories
f. providing misinformation about facts (euphemism for lying).
g. submitting tampered evidence
h. making ridiculous claims
i. stalling to delay proceedings

j. obstruction of justice

D. REMEDIES

Judgment by default must be entered against Defendant Toala. Find Attorney McCann in contempt of court, have him arrested, and incarcerated until discovery requested in Plaintiff's Interrogatories is delivered. In addition, find Attorney Cardozo in contempt of court and order him to provide discovery material requested by Plaintiff before September, 15, 2009. If discovery material is not delivered before September 15, 2009, Judge Koeltl should award requested damages to Plaintiff by September 18, 2009.

No extensions of the September 15, 2009, submission date should be allowed. If the trial is to continue, the Clerk of Court should provide a calendar of proceedings to trial by September 22, 2009, in which the trial must be completed by January 31, 2010. This calendar must include dates for the following:

a. Revised Complaint returned to Plaintiff for service of summons to new list of defendants. Plaintiff will submit revised complaint to the Court on October 1, 2009.
b. Response to request by Plaintiff to the Clerk of Court for the jury selection information requested
c. List of jury pool names and other pertinent information
d. Jury selection
e. Procedure for *voir dire*
f. Service of *subpoenas*
g. Individual interviews of all defendants and other witnesses
h. Possible dates for the jury trial

E. MOTIONS

Plaintiff moves that Judge Koeltl find Attorney McCann in contempt of court, have him arrested, and incarcerated until discovery requested in Plaintiff's Interrogatories is delivered.

Plaintiff moves that Judge Koeltl, in addition, find Attorney Cardozo in contempt and to provide discovery material requested by Plaintiff before September, 15, 2009. Plaintiff moves that, if discovery material is not delivered before September 15, 2009, Judge Koeltl should award requested damages to Plaintiff by September 18, 2009.

Plaintiff moves that Judge Koeltl, in addition, find Attorney Cardozo in contempt and to provide discovery material requested by Plaintiff before September, 15, 2009.

Plaintiff moves that, if discovery material is not delivered before September 15, 2009, Judge Koeltl should award requested damages to Plaintiff by September 18, 2009.

XXIII. MISUSE OF COURT RULES

On September 3, 2009 I submitted a:

MEMORANDUM OF LAW: MISUSE OF COURT RULES

A. PREAMBLE

The U. S. District Court of the Southern District of New York routinely violates its own rules. Specific examples follow below. Citations given by number and/or Exhibit number refer to the reference number (1 or 2), and its item number, and/or exhibit number, respectively, in the two references given at the end of this memorandum in Section J.

B. LATE ENTRY OF DEFENDANT TOALA

On March 2, 2009 Defendants Toala and Kelly were served (2-63). On March 25, 2009 Attorneys Michael A. Cardozo and Max McCann filed a **NOTICE OF APPEARANCE** for Defendant Kelly, but not Defendant Toala.

On April 2, 2009, Plaintiff moved to close proceedings on Defendants Toala and Kelly. On April 16, 2009, Judge Koeltl denied Plaintiff's motion to close pleadings for Defendants Toala and Kelly on the grounds that those Defendants have not yet answered the complaint. He states that in his April 2, 2009, **ORDER** he extended the time for Defendants who have been served to respond until May 15, 2009. On July 17, 2009, Attorneys McCann and Cardozo made an entry for Defendant Toala, 3-1/2 months after it was due.

Based on FRCP 4(a)(1) (E), the summons served on Defendants Toala and Kelly reads, in part:

> "**SUMMONS IN A CIVIL ACTION** To: (Defendant's name and address) A lawsuit has been filed against you. Within 20 days after service of this summons on you (not counting the day you received it) or 60 days if you are the United States or a United States agency, or an officer or employee of the United States described in Fed. R. Civ. P. 12 (a)(2) or (3) you must serve on the plaintiff an answer to the attached complaint or a motion under Rule 12 of the Federal Rules of Civil Procedure. The answer or motion must be served on the plaintiff or plaintiff's attorney, whose name and address are: _______. If you fail to respond, judgment by default will be entered against you for the relief demanded in the complaint. You also must file your answer or motion with the court."

Notice that the above statement says the judgment by default will (not may) be entered against you. The only exceptions are given in Federal rules of Civil Procedure (FRCP) Rule 6 (1) which states:

> "(1) In General. When an act may or must be done within a specified time, the court may, for good cause, extend the time: with or without motion or notice if the court acts, or if a request is made, before the original time or its extension expires; or (B) on motion made after the time has expired if the party failed to act because of excusable neglect."

Neither of these exceptions are applicable here. Therefore the Court must render judgment against Defendant Toala. At the conference of July 17, 2009, Plaintiff mentioned the late entry of defense counsel for Defendant Toala and asked that the Court issue judgment against him. Judge Koeltl's response was:

> "...default judgments are not favored in the court. If a defendant shows up and is prepared to litigate, the court favors cases being litigated on their merits."

C. AIDING DISCOVERY

Plaintiff received a copy of a letter dated March 19, 2009, from Max McCann, Counsel for Raymond Kelly, in the above-named case. He requested "...that the Court order Plaintiff to provide an executed consent and authorization for the release of medical records and records that may have been sealed pursuant to New York Criminal Procedure Law #160.50." (1-22: Exhibit 16)

On March 27, 2009, Plaintiff replied to the *Pro Se* Office of the U. S. District Court for the Southern District of New York concerning the correspondence of March 19, 2009, from Max McCann. In that correspondence, Petitioner stated that:

> "I find it curious that the police have lied to me three times, failed to submit waiver of summons forms, and failed to supply the names of John Does 1, 2 & 3, but expect me to fulfill their requests. Furthermore Judge Keiltl (sic) has failed to act on three motions that I submitted on February 28, 2009. One of these was for a jury trial, a simple request that he cannot deny. A second one was for a time delay for responding to informations submitted in March, 2009, which is now moot. The third motion was to order Defendants Toala and Kelly to provide identification information for the John Does."

On April 2, 2009, Paralegal Nicole Wright sent two separate letters, one with additional copies of release forms to Petitioner. On April 2, 2009, Judge Koeltl issued an **ORDER** stating that there is no need to move for a jury trial, denying Plaintiff's request for an extension of time to respond, denying the request to have defendants pay for service, and denying a motion for ordering the defendants to identify the John Doe Defendants. Also, he directed the Plaintiff to execute the releases for medical records and to provide executed releases concerning Plaintiff's arrest. In addition he granted Defendants an extension of time to respond to the complaint to May 15, 2009.

On April 6, 2009, Plaintiff submitted Interrogatories to Defendants Toala and Kelly to send names and identifying information for the five defendants; Persons whose arrest were allegedly impeded by Plaintiff; Pedestrians whose passage was allegedly impeded by Plaintiff; and the lady, identified as a nurse, who pleaded with police on behalf of Plaintiff at the demonstration of April 17, 2007. Accompanying this request were motions for the Court to order the Defendants to comply. Copies were sent to the *Pro Se* Office of the U. S. District Court for the Southern District of New York.

On April 14, 2009, the *Pro Se* Clerk of the U. S. District Court for the Southern District of New York returned Exhibits 7 and 8 of reference 2 to Plaintiff stating that pursuant to Rule 5.1(a) discovery materials cannot be accepted for filing with the Court. Plaintiff sent these forms twice to Mr. McCann; once on April 6, 2009; and once on April 20, 2009 (2-69).

On April 17, 2009, the *Pro Se* Clerk of the U. S. District Court for the Southern District of New York sent a letter to Plaintiff informing him that after he obtains the identity of the John Doe Defendants, he will have to file a newly amended complaint. He also advised Plaintiff that pursuant to the Court's April 1, 2009, Order Plaintiff must promptly execute the releases of medical and criminal records.

On April 20, 2009, Plaintiff executed a **DESIGNATION OF AGENT FOR ACCESS TO SEALED RECORDS** form in the presence of a notary public. On May 5, 2009 the *Pro Se* Office of the U. S. District Court for the Southern District of New York returned Plaintiff's courtesy copy of the **DESIGNATION OF AGENT FOR ACCESS TO SEALED RECORDS**.

Attorney McCann was not satisfied with either of Plaintiff's two responses to the Interrogatory. On May 8, 2009, Attorney Max McCann wrote to Judge Koeltl to again request Plaintiff to complete the consent and authorization prepared by his office for the release of records, and for a second extension of time to respond to Plaintiff's Complaint. He filed a Motion with Judge Koeltl to order Plaintiff to complete the interrogatory exactly as submitted. On May 9, 2009, Judge Koeltl issued such an **ORDER**. So much for the Court not aiding in discovery.

On May 12, 2009, Judge Koeltl issued an **ORDER** directing plaintiff to provide counsel for defense the consent and authorization for the release of sealed records that has been provided by Attorney McCann. He also extended the time for defendants to respond until June 26, 2009.

On June 12, 2009, Mr. McMann sent a letter to Judge Koeltl requesting dismissal of the case because "Plaintiff has not submitted an executed or release of records that may have been sealed pursuant to New York Criminal Procedure Law #160.50."

On June 16, 2009, Judge Koeltl issued an **ORDER** instructing parties to appear at a conference on June 26, 2009. On June 22, 2009, Plaintiff informed Judge Koeltl that he would be out-of-town on June 26, 2009, and suggested some other dates. On June 26, 2009, Judge Koeltl issued an **ORDER** to move the date of the conference from June 26, 2009, to July 17, 2009, to accommodate Plaintiff's travel schedule. He directs Plaintiff to provide the authorizations to Defense Counsel by July 10, 2009. Apparently Judge Koeltl refuses to accept the fact that this already had been done twice.

On July 28, 2009, Plaintiff sent a letter to Max McCann with an Interrogatory requesting the identity of all police officers at the confrontation with Plaintiff on April 17, 2007; of the nurse who aided Plaintiff; any known witnesses; all persons whose arrest allegedly was interfered by Plaintiff; and all persons whose pedestrian or vehicular passage was allegedly impeded by Plaintiff.

A summary of the Court's aid to defendants' discovery is:

a. Requests for **DESIGNATION OF AGENT FOR ACCESS TO SEALED RECORDS** were sent to Plaintiff by Defendants by mail five times (March 19, April 2 [2 letters from Paralegal Nicole Wright], May 8, 2009; and May 12, 2009). The last two letters were sent after Defendants had received the completed designation.
b. Judge Koeltl issued **ORDERS** and requests to Plaintiff five times (April 2, 2009; May 9, 2009; May 12, 2009; June 16, 2009; and June 26, 2009) to submit the designation. Four of these **ORDERS** and requests were made after Plaintiff had submitted the designation.
c. On April 14, 2009, the *Pro Se* Clerk advised Plaintiff that pursuant to the Court's April 1, 2009 Order Plaintiff must promptly execute the releases of medical and criminal records. This request was made after Plaintiff had made the first submission.
d. Plaintiff had submitted the designation forms twice (April 6, 2009, and April 20, 2009). Between submissions Plaintiff received a telephone call from Mr. McCann stating that the first submission was unsatisfactory.
e. On May 5, 2009, the *Pro Se* Clerk returned Plaintiff's courtesy copy of the release form which he submitted to the Court.

A summary of the Court's refusal to aid Plaintiff's discovery is:

a. Plaintiff submitted three Interrogatories (February 8, 2009; April 6, 2009; and July 28, 2009) to Defendants asking them to identify the John Doe police officers who were listed as Defendants.

b. On April 14, 2009, the *Pro Se* Clerk returned Plaintiff's interrogatory of April 6, 2009 with the statement "Pursuant to Rule 5.1(a) of the Local Rules for the Southern District of New York, discovery materials cannot be accepted for filing with the Court."

c. Plaintiff submitted motions three times (February 28, 2009; April 6, 2009; August 28, 2009) to the Court asking for an **ORDER** on defendants to respond to the interrogatories. The first motion was denied by Judge Koeltl. The second motion was returned to Plaintiff with the statement that the Court does not aid in discovery. There has been no response to the third motion.

D. REFUSAL TO RESPOND TO INTERROGATORIES

Discovery disclosure is required as stated in Rule 26: Duty to Disclose; General Provisions Governing Discovery. Rule 26(a)(1)(A) states:

(a) Required Disclosures. (1) Initial Disclosures. (A) In General. Except as exempted by Rule 26(a)(1)(B) or as otherwise stipulated or ordered by the court, a party must, without awaiting a discovery request, provide to the other parties:

(i) the name and, if known, the address and telephone number of each individual likely to have discoverable information "along with the subjects of that information" that the disclosing party may use to

> support its claims or defenses, unless the use would be solely for impeachment;

Three times Plaintiff submitted Interrogatories to Attorney McCann to produce discovery material (February 28, 2009; April 6, 2009, and July 27, 2009). Each interrogatory has been ignored (2-76). After each Interrogatory was submitted, Plaintiff submitted motions to order Defendants to respond to the interrogatories. (February 28, 2009; April 6, 2009; and August 28, 2009).

The first motion was denied by Judge Koeltl on the flimsy reason that not enough information was available. Did Judge Koeltl really believe that Defendant Toala did not know which police officers assisted him in the kidnapping? The second motion was returned to Plaintiff by the Clerk of Court with the statement that the Court does not aid in discovery. No action has been taken by the Court on the third set of motions.

E. EXTENSION OF RESPONSE TIMES

On February 28, 2009, I sent a cover letter and three motions to the *Pro Se* Office. The three motions were:

a. Motion for a jury trial
b. Motion for a response time after April 15, 2009, for any informations submitted in March, 2009
c. Motion for identity of John Does

On April 2, 2009, of Judge Koeltl issued an **ORDER** stating that there is no need to move for a jury trial, denying Plaintiff's request for an extension of time to respond, denying the request to have defendants pay for service, and denying a motion for ordering the defendants to identify the John Doe Defendants. Also, he directed the Plaintiff to execute the releases for medical records and to provide executed releases concerning Plaintiff's arrest.

On June 12, 2009, Max McCann sent a letter to Judge Koeltl complaining (incorrectly) that Plaintiff has not provided the executed consent and authorization for the release of records that may have been sealed pursuant to NYCPL #160.50. He requested that plaintiff's complaint be dismissed pursuant to FRCP 16(f). 41 (b) and 37(b)(2)(C).

On June 16, Judge Koeltl issued an **ORDER** for a conference among the parties on June 26, 2009 (Exhibit B). To accommodate Plaintiff's travel schedule (Exhibit C), the conference date was changed to July 17, 2009 (2-22).

On July 20, 2009, Judge Koeltl issued an order giving defendants time to move or answer is extended to July 31, 2009. Any motion to stay the defendants' wish to file must also be filed by July 31, 2009. "The plaintiff's response to any motion to stay is due by August 14, 2009. The defendants may reply by August 24, 2009."

On August 18, 2009, Judge Koeltl issued an **ORDER** advising Plaintiff to submit a response and affidavits by September 4, 2009. Defendant's reply date is September 18, 2009. The original response time for Defendants was 30 days after receiving the summons of March 2, 2009. Thus it would be April 2, 2009. However response time extensions were given by Judge Koeltl as follows:

a. The initial response time of 30 days to answer the summons of March 2, 2009, was April 2, 2009.
b. On April 2, 2009, the date was extended to May 15, 2009.
c. On May 12, 2009, the date was extended to June 26, 2009.
d. On July 20, 2009, the date to move was extended to July 31, 2009.

e. On July 20, 2009, the date to reply was extended to August 24, 2009.
f. On August 18, 2009, the date was extended to September 18, 2009.

No time extension requests of Mr. McCann were refused.

Plaintiff made two requests for time extensions. One was denied, and one was granted. These were:

a. On February 28, 2009, Plaintiff requested a time extension until April 15, 2009 to response to any informations he might receive, because he would be out of town from March 3–22, 2009. On April 2, 2009, Judge Koeltl refused Plaintiff's request for a time extension to April 15, 2009.
b. On June 26, 2009, Judge Koeltl issued an **ORDER** to move the date of the conference from June 26, 2009, to July 17, 2009, to accommodate Plaintiff's travel schedule.

F. REFUSING INFORMATIONS FOR THE CASE RECORD

On April 14, 2009, the *Pro Se* Clerk of the U. S. District Court for the Southern District of New York returned Exhibits 7 and 8 of reference 2 to Plaintiff stating that pursuant to Rule 5.1(a) discovery materials cannot be accepted for filing with the Court. On May 5, 2009, the *Pro Se* Office of the U. S. District Court for the Southern District of New York returned Plaintiff's courtesy copy of the **DESIGNATION OF AGENT FOR ACCESS TO SEALED RECORDS**.

The second motion was returned to Plaintiff by the Clerk of Court with the statement that the Court does not aid in discovery. A letter of *Pro Se* Office of the U. S. District Court of Southern

New York to Plaintiff of August 4, 2009, returned Interrogatories of July 28, 2009.

G. VIOLATION OF FORMAT RULE

In my letter of August 8, 2009, I point out that Local Civil Rule 56.1 (a) states:

> "Upon any motion for summary judgment pursuant to Rule 56 of the Federal Rules of Civil Procedure, there shall be annexed to the notice of motion a separate, short and concise statement, in numbered paragraphs, of the material facts as to which the moving party contends there is no genuine issue to be tried. Failure to submit such a statement may constitute grounds for denial of the motion."

Since Mr. McCann failed to follow this rule, this is grounds for the rejection of his **MEMORANDUM OF LAW AND DENIAL OF THE MOTION** based on this memorandum. However Judge Koeltl did not do this.

H. VIOLATIONS OF RULES

In summary, the rules with which the Court did not comply are summarized as:

a. FRCP 4(a)(1)(E) not enforced: reply time after service.
b. Court does not enforce discovery rule FRCP 26(a)(1)(A) on Defendants.
c. Court continues to give unwarranted extensions of time to Defendants to answer complaint. Defendants submit unfounded requests for time extensions for the purpose of delaying trial until the Plaintiff dies. Some of their

requests contain misinformation and even a tampered DVD video made by the police.

d. Court does not accept submissions of Plaintiff based on Rule 5.1(a) discovery materials cannot be accepted for filing with the Court. It used this rule to return Motion requests, information about jury procedures, interrogatories, and release forms. Meanwhile Judge Koeltl is issuing **ORDERS** to Plaintiff to deliver discovery materials which either do not exist or which have already been delivered to Defendants.

e. Defendants did not follow the format required by Local Civil Rule 56.1 (a) with impunity when they submitted their **MEMORANDUM OF LAW** for dismissal based on the DVD video evidence.

XXIV. REPLY OF DEFENDANTS

The Defendants responded to my Memorandum of Law, and Judge Koeltl issued an **ORDER.** I wrote to Judge Koeltl on October 19, 2009, as follows:

"I am responding to your **ORDER** of September 22, 2009, in response to Mr. McCann's letter of September 18, 2009. In Mr. McCann's letter he states that defendants have not been served with a motion for summary judgment. Presumably he is referring to the three motions on page 23 of my **MEMORANDUM OF LAW IN SUPPORT OF CONTEMPT PROCEEDINGS AGAINST COUNSELS FOR DEFENSE MICHAEL A. CARDOZO AND MAX MCCANN** of August 28, 2009."

"His claim is false. The interrogatory to which he must respond is enclosed. It was sent to him by certified mail on July 28, 2009. A copy of the signed certified receipt is attached."

"Accompanying the Memorandum of Law of August 28, 2009, was a letter addressed to Judge Koeltl, Affidavit of Plaintiff, Notice of Motion, Affirmation in Support of Motion, and Affirmation of Service. These documents were all mailed to Messrs. Cardozo and McCann on August 28, 2009, by certified U. S. mail. Copies of the signed certified receipts are attached."

"The Defense also is asking for dismissal of the case based on the video evidence and the **REPLY MEMORANDUM OF LAW IN FURTHER SUPPORT OF DEFENDANTS' MOTION TO DISMISS OR, IN THE ALTERNATIVE, FOR SUMMARY JUDGMENT** of September 18, 2009. Before responding to this, I remind you that any dispute about the facts must be resolved by the jury, not by a judge nor either litigant's counsels. That is the duty of the jury. Furthermore during discovery, the movant must prove his contentions **BEYOND ANY**

DOUBT. CLOSE TO BEYOND ANY DOUBT IS NOT GOOD ENOUGH."

"A detailed response to the Memorandum of Law of Messrs. Cardozo and McCann of September 18, 2009, is enclosed in my Memorandum of Law of October 19, 2009."

"My current travel schedule is: October 28–31, 2009: Lancaster, PA, December 2-21, 2009: Cupertino and Palm Springs, CA. Please do not schedule any court dates during those periods. Thanks."

"It has been terrifying to learn that the corporation counsels for New York City do not know the law, cannot understand the meaning of court cases, do not know the rules of evidence, do not follow court rules, do not understand English, and cannot tell the truth. You have let them make a farce out of this trial. They should be disbarred from practicing law."

"Perhaps you are of the same persuasion as they. Your behavior has been shameful. I have filed judicial complaints against you with the New York State Supreme Court, Appellate Division, First Judicial Department, Department Disciplinary Committee and the United States Court of Appeals: Second Circuit. Also I filed a criminal complaint against you with the U. S. Attorney for obstruction of justice. You have been unwilling to conduct a fair and impartial trial. I have lost all trust in your decisions."

"I move that you recuse yourself from presiding over this trial, and have a new judge appointed. Notice of Motion, Affirmation in Support of Motion, and Affirmation of Service are enclosed."

"Do not return this letter nor any of the accompanying documents. Add them to the case record. If there is a rule against this, ignore the rule."

XXV. RESPONSE TO DEFENDANTS

I submitted a **RESPONSE MEMORANDUM OF LAW TO REPLY MEMORANDUM OF LAW IN FURTHER SUPPORT OF DEFENDANTS' MOTION TO DISMISS OR, IN THE ALTERNATIVE, FOR SUMMARY JUDGMENT** as follows:

A. INTRODUCTION

The Defense is asking for dismissal of the case based on the video evidence and the **REPLY MEMORANDUM OF LAW IN FURTHER SUPPORT OF DEFENDANTS' MOTION TO DISMISS OR, IN THE ALTERNATIVE, FOR SUMMARY JUDGMENT** of September 18, 2009. Before responding to this, Plaintiff reminds the Judge that he may not rule on the facts. That is the duty of the jury. Furthermore during discovery the movant must prove his contentions **BEYOND ANY DOUBT. CLOSE TO BEYOND ANY DOUBT IS NOT GOOD ENOUGH.**

THE VIDEO TIMELINE

The video timeline is:

0:06 Police blue shield appears.
0:25 Lieutenant Wolf announces that he is on the bullhorn.
0:40 Demonstrators ordered to clear the steps and sidewalk or be arrested.
0:50 Plaintiff is seen standing behind the sitting demonstrators.
1:38 Another picture of Plaintiff standing behind the sitting demonstrators.
2:25 Picture of standing demonstrators with pedestrians moving by unobstructed.

2:43 The sitting demonstrators ordered to leave the staircase or be arrested for disorderly conduct. Plaintiff is not in the picture.
2:53 Plaintiff is shown standing behind the sitting demonstrators who are ordered to leave or be arrested. Nobody has been arrested yet.
3:05 Plaintiff is shown standing at the head of the standing demonstrators.
3:19 & 3:37: Pedestrians are escorted by the police through the sitting demonstrators.
3:45 First sitting demonstrators taken into custody.
4:05 Plaintiff is not in the picture.
4:22 Plaintiff is not among the sitting demonstrators.
5:07 Warning that if you do not want to be arrested, clear the stairs now. Plaintiff is not in the picture.
5:14 Warning is given by police that all sitting demonstrators will be arrested.
6:29 Warning that remaining sitting demonstrators must clear the steps now or be arrested also.
7:22 Plaintiff is shown standing alone well behind the sitting demonstrators. A police officer is standing right behind the sitting demonstrators.
7:28 There is a full shot of the Plaintiff holding signs, but not making body movement or saying anything. Pedestrian traffic is not blocked.
7:34 A pedestrian walks by Plaintiff unimpeded.
7:54 There is a free flow of pedestrian traffic through the last several sitting demonstrators.
9:06 There is shot of the last 6 sitting demonstrators. Plaintiff is not in the picture.
11:00 Last sitting demonstrator is removed.
11:10 Sidewalk and stairs are cleared. Pedestrians walk by.
11:19 Police Approach standing Plaintiff.

11:25 There is conversation between the police officer and Plaintiff that is not audible (presumably deleted from the video).
11:33 Another police officer joins the first police officer and Plaintiff.
11:39 Plaintiff falls down for no apparent reason (sound has been deleted from the video).
11:47 A woman approaches Plaintiff (who identified herself as a nurse, but this statement is not on the video).
11:50 A pedestrian easily passes Plaintiff, who is still on the ground motionless.
11:56 Five police officers (one in plain clothes) around Plaintiff. One says to call 911.
12:00 Another police officer approaches.
12:06 The plain clothes officer leaves.
12:31 Police call for a carry detail.
12:41 Nurse asks the police why Plaintiff is being arrested. It appears that Plaintiff is unconscious.
12:50 There are about 5 police officers near Plaintiff. The sound track is muffled.
13:24 Plaintiff starts to rise.
13:38 There is a muffled conversation.
13:49 Plaintiff informs police that he has a permit to be there.
14:03 Plaintiff reads Amendment I from his pocket U. S. Constitution.
14:30 Plaintiff warns police that if arrested, they will be sued.
14:36 Plaintiff lies down again.
14:44 Plaintiff voices vociferous objection.
14:48 Police start dragging Plaintiff away.
14:54 Officer says that Plaintiff should be charged with resisting arrest.
16:00 Six police officers carry Plaintiff away.
16:25 A police officer announces that the time is 13:05 (1:05 pm).

17:08 Officer Rivera announce that the demonstration is concluded.

The video has some interesting features:

a. Some of the sound track is muffled, and some is missing.
b. Nowhere in the video is Plaintiff placed under arrest.
c. An old man falls to the ground and is motionless and speechless. The normal reaction is to assume that he has had a stroke or heart attack. An ambulance should be called. At 11:56 one police officer suggests calling 911, but his suggestion is ignored.
d. Only the sitting demonstrators were arrested. No standing demonstrators were arrested. Plaintiff was never sitting at any time during the demonstration, but he was singled out for arrest.
e. At 14:54 an officer says that Plaintiff should be charged with resisting arrest. This is a remarkable statement, since Plaintiff cannot be resisting arrest, if he has not been placed under arrest.
f. In any event a person lying on the ground who is motionless and speechless cannot be resisting arrest. He may be unconscious or dead.

Perhaps this can be clarified if we examine Officer Toala's deposition, which is Exhibit A. The deposition states:

a. Deponent Toala states that he placed the Plaintiff under arrest (not detention) for several listed crimes by Plaintiff at or about 12:51 hours.
b. At 16:25 on the tape, a police officer announces the time to be 1:05 pm.

c. Thus Plaintiff was placed under "arrest" 14 minutes earlier, or at 2:25 on the tape time. There is no possibility of this being true.
d. Either Deponent Toala is mistaken (lying) or a significant part of the tape is missing.
e. It would not be surprising if Deponent Toala is lying, since every other allegation in the deposition is false. However there seems to be no logical reason for Deponent Toala to lie about the time of "arrest."
f. We must conclude that part of the video is missing.

Let us examine the reasons given for arrest in the deposition:

a. "Deponent observed the defendant lying/sitting on the floor at the above location on the steps and sidewalk." This does not occur in the video until after police officers apprehended Plaintiff.
b. "blocking the normal flow of pedestrian traffic and obstructing pedestrian traffic as follows: pedestrians had to walk around the defendant and pedestrians were unable to access stairs and access to the above location." This never occurs anywhere in the video.
c. Defendants' conduct created a public disturbance/ inconvenience in that it caused a crowd to gather, disruption of the normal flow of traffic, and people to express alarm." None of this occurs in the video when Plaintiff is standing alone. It only happens after he is accosted and surrounded by police. The police caused the public disturbance, and are the ones who should have been arrested.
d. "Deponent further states that when he was placing the defendant under arrest for the offense(s) describe above defendant (sic) the defendant laid on the steps and

> refused to stand up and place defendant's hands behind defendant's back." Even if this were true, it cannot be a cause of arrest since it would have happened after Plaintiff was placed under arrest.

Some of the sound in the video is missing. The missing part is described in Plaintiff's attached statement, which was written on April 18, 2007, immediately after arriving home from the arraignment hearing. It was updated on April 19, 2007, (two days after the incident) at 4:55 pm, just after Plaintiff returned from taking measurements at the scene of the incident. The typographical errors in the original have not been corrected to preserve authenticity.

Plaintiff's statement points out that the unintelligible sound on the video was the point at which Plaintiff was placed under arrest two times. (The police had rescinded the first notice of arrest.) Plaintiff asked the reason for the arrest and was told for failing to obey an order of the police. No other reason was given. Then Plaintiff fell to the ground for the second time. He remained motionless and mute until the medics approached him in the cell at police headquarters.

Plaintiff's statement provides a somewhat different view of events. In particular, when Plaintiff asked the police officers why he was being placed under arrest, the only reason given was for refusing to obey the order of a law enforcement official. This is not a legitimate cause for arrest. If officers told Plaintiff to jump off a cliff, and he refused, would the refusal be a cause of arrest?

Any dispute about the facts must be resolved by the jury, not by a judge nor either litigant's counsels.

POINT I: PLAINTIFF CANNOT STATE A CLAIM FOR PURPORTED VIOLATIONS OF NEW YORK PENAL LAW

Defendants claim that Plaintiff has attempted to state a claim against defendants for alleged infractions of New York State Penal Law. This statement is false. Plaintiff has charged Defendants in his complaint for violation of his Constitutional rights under Amendments I and XIV of the U. S. Constitution. In several documents Plaintiff also claims that Defendants have violated numerous New York State penal laws. These are:

a. Kidnapping by Defendants Toala, Commissioner Kelly, and several John Doe police officers Section 135.25 P2 (d) Kidnapping in the first degree
b. Reckless endangerment by Officer Toala, Section 120.15 Menacing in the third degree
c. Ordered to commit a crime by Officer Toala, New York Penal Code: Section 1.05 General purposes 1. To proscribe conduct which unjustifiably and inexcusably causes or threatens substantial harm to individual or public interests;
d. Perjury by Officer Toala, and Counsels McCann and Cardozo. TITLE 18 > PART I > CHAPTER 79 > §1621 (1)
e. Obstruction of justice by Defendants Toala and Kelly, Counsels Cardozo and McCann, Judge Koeltl, and Clerks of the U. S. District Court McMahon and Marmolejos; Section 1.05 General purposes.
f. Tampering with the video by deleting critical parts by Defendants Toala and Kelly and other unnamed police personnel. New York Penal Code: Section 1.05 General Purposes 1. To proscribe conduct which unjustifiably and inexcusably causes or threatens substantial harm to individual or public interests.

g. Theft of demonstration signs by arresting police officers and other unnamed police personnel; New York Penal Code: Section 155.05 Larceny (1)

Defendants point out that in Luckett v. Bure, the case was dismissed because no federal law violation was invoked. However New York State laws are not the basis for the present civil suit. The basis for the civil suit is violation of Amendments I and XIV of the U. S. Constitution. The New York State laws indicate how Plaintiff's First Amendment rights were violated.

POINT II. PLAINTIFF FAILS TO SUFFICIENTLY ALLEGE THAT DEFENDANT COMMISSIONER KELLY WAS PERSONALLY INVOLVED IN HIS ARREST

It is not required of the moved party (Plaintiff) to support his allegations or lack thereof. It is required that the movant prove beyond any doubt that Defendant Kelly was not involved [Conley v. Gibson, 355 U.S. 41 (1957)]. Almost no doubt does not qualify [Anderson v. Creighton, 483 U.S. 635 at 644 (1987); Jenkins v. City of New York, 478 F. 3d at 87, 2d Cir. (2007)]. Plaintiff's claim that Defendant Kelly was involved are based on both the specific actions of the police at the incident and because of repeated general behavior of the police.

Specific actions of the police

The demonstration was publicized widely well in advance. It was covered by all types of media and received worldwide coverage. It was organized by Rabbi Avi Weiss, one of the most highly respected rabbis in the U. S. It is clear that the arrests were well orchestrated in advance. Present were many police officers, including those from the Patrol Boro Manhattan South Task Force and legal advisors.

The rabbis congregated on the stairs and gave speeches without police interference. The rabbis sat on the stairs and were ordered to move several times before being placed under arrest. After the arrests, a John Doe Officer announced on a bullhorn that the demonstration was over.

It is not the prerogative of the police to end a peaceful demonstration. Plaintiff alleges that this would not have been done without Commissioner Kelly's permission.

In order to end the demonstration the police had moved all the standing demonstrators 35 feet back, so that they could not be seen from the street. None of the standing demonstrators, except Plaintiff, were arrested.

Plaintiff originally had moved back 35 feet with the other standing demonstrators, but when he realized that he could not be seen from the street, he moved forward 22 feet, but still 13 feet behind the sitting demonstrators. Plaintiff was ordered to move back with the other standing demonstrators or be arrested. After some discussion with the police, he was placed "under arrest."

General criminal behavior of police

The New York City Police probably are the largest criminal syndicate in the United States. They commit homicide (Exhibits C1- C9), sodomize arrestees (Exhibits C10-C11), rape (Exhibits 12 & 13), commit robbery (Exhibit C14), assault (Exhibits C15-C17), theft (Exhibit C18 & C22), false detainments (Exhibits C19 & C23), reckless endangerment (Exhibit C20), use excessive force (Exhibit C21), distribute illegal narcotics (Exhibit C19 & C22), and harass innocent citizens (Exhibit C23).

Bernard Kerick, Police Commissioner of New York City from 2000-2001 during the Giuliani "law and order" administration, committed several crimes. In 2006, Kerik pled guilty to two unrelated ethics violations after an investigation by the Bronx District Attorney's Office, and was ordered to pay

$221,000. A grand jury issued a multi-count indictment on November 8, 2007, alleging conspiracy, mail fraud, wire fraud and lying to the Internal Revenue Service.

As far as Plaintiff knows, the New York City Police have not published their narcotic inventories recently, which is suspicion that some narcotics are currently missing. Other police departments, as well as U. S. border guards, have been implicated in the illegal narcotics trade.

Burden of Proof

During discovery, the burden of proof is on the moving party. The moved party is not obligated to prove anything until trial. At the present time, Plaintiff admits that he has not proved his allegation, but he is not required to do so during discovery.

Cardozo and McCann argue that Plaintiff's claim that Defendant Kelly was involved is insufficient to state a claim for which relief may be granted. They argue that Plaintiff fails to plead sufficient facts to allege that defendant Kelly was personally involved. They site Goldstein et al. v. Pataki et al., 516 F.3d 50 (2d Cir. 2008) as a reference.

Goldstein et al. made an eminent domain claim. It involved a question of law, not of facts. There was a public hearing, not a trial, where the claims were a violation of Amendments V and XIV of the U. S. Constitution.

Plaintiffs claimed that their properties were taken improperly under eminent domain, because the "claims of public benefit are a pretext" to help the developer. Plaintiffs sued in District Court. The District Court held that a pretext argument was a valid basis for a public-use challenge under Supreme Court's decision in Kelo v. City of New London, 545 U.S. 469 (2005), but was not available here, because even if Plaintiffs could prove every allegation, a reasonable juror would not be able to conclude that the public use offered in the support of the project were mere pretexts.

Plaintiffs conceded that the ESDC had at all times abided by the letter of the strict requirements of the state law. A motion to dismiss was granted, accepting all factual allegations as true, and drawing all reasonable inferences in plaintiff's favor.

The Court quoted Conley v. Gibson, 355 U.S/ 41 (1957) that a complaint cannot be dismissed unless it appears that Plaintiff cannot prove it (127 S. Ct. at 1968-quoting Conley,355 U. S. at 45,46). At trial, the District Court decided that the claim could not be proved and dismissed the case. (Heicklen's comment: This is a distressing statement. The Court is usurping the prerogative of the jury to make that decision.) The Circuit Court of Appeals upheld the decision of the District Court.

Conclusion

It is not incumbent on the moved party to prove or even substantiate a claim during discovery. It is incumbent on the movant to disprove the claim beyond any doubt. The Defendants in the present case have not done this, or even offered an argument in its favor.

POINT III: THERE WAS PROBABLE CAUSE FOR PLAINTIFF'S ARREST

On Page 3 of Cardozo and McCann, they state that "Plaintiff also argues that police officers did not have probable cause to arrest him because 'he had read Amendment I of the U. S. Constitution to the police officers, so that they were well aware that they were violating his constitutional rights.'" Again Cardozo and McCann misstate Plaintiff's position. The police were not violating Plaintiff's Constitutional rights because he read them anything. They were violating his rights if he had said nothing at all. Plaintiff was just informing them of that fact, so that they would be aware of it, and not be able to declare immunity.

Cardozo and McCann further state: "Here plaintiff erroneously assumes that his subjective determination as to the scope of his constitutional rights is the standard by which probable cause is judged." They lied again. It is not Plaintiff's standard. It is the standard established in Amendment I of the U. S. Constitution. Plaintiff understands English. Apparently Messrs. Cardozo and McCann do not.

Cardozo and McCann state that "In Startzell v. City of Philadelphia, Pennsylvania 533 F.3d 183, 204 (3d Cir. 2008), plaintiffs claimed that they could not be arrested for disorderly conduct because they were exercising their right to free speech." However Plaintiffs Startzell et al. were not arrested for exercising their right to free speech, but for disorderly conduct, because they were interfering with and trying to break up a rally by a group which had a permit to be there. This is entirely different from the present case.

Startzell states: "The burden is on the City to demonstrate the constitutionality of its actions." Startzell states: "Equally obvious is it that a State may not unduly suppress free communication of views, religious or other, under the guise of conserving desirable conditions."

"The Supreme Court reached similar conclusions in Cox v. Louisiana, 379 U. S. 536, 551 (1965) and Terminello, 337 U. S. at 5. In both cases the Court overturned convictions for 'breaching the peace' where state law defined that crime as encompassing, respectively, (1) 'to interrupt, to hinder, to disquiet,' and (2) 'speech that invites dispute or create a disturbance.'"

"Furthermore Parks, 195 F.3d at 652; see also Grace, 461, U. S. at 180 stating that government "may not by its own *ipse dixit* destroy the 'public forum' status of streets and parks which have historically been public forums.""

Carey v. Brown, 447 U. S. 455, 460 (1980) states: "Streets, sidewalks, parks, and other similar public places are so historically associated with the exercise of First Amendment rights that access to them for the purpose of exercising such rights cannot constitutionally be denied broadly and absolutely."

On page 4, Cardozo and McCann lied again when they stated: "Instead they issued a lawful order to disperse to a crowd that, by plaintiff's own admission, was blocking traffic." First it is impossible to disperse to a crowd. This is an oxymoron. Second, Plaintiff was ordered to congregate with the crowd which was blocking pedestrian traffic. An order to join a crowd that is committing a crime cannot be lawful. Another oxymoron.

Messrs. Cardozo and McCann further state: "Further, it is undisputed that Plaintiff refused to comply with an order to disperse." Another lie. Plaintiff certainly does dispute that he was ordered to disperse. He was ordered to congregate.

Cardozo and McCann further state: "While Plaintiff does not contest the fact that he was part of a crowd that was ordered to disperse," Two more lies. Plaintiff was not part of a crowd. He was standing alone. The crowd was not ordered to disperse. It remained after Plaintiff was dragged away. Nobody in that crowd was arrested.

Messrs. Cardozo and McCann continue with "Plaintiff appears to argue that, once police have arrested all other individuals for refusing to disperse the last person remaining is protected from arrest." Another lie. Plaintiff never argued any such thing. The police ordered the sitting demonstrators to stand or be arrested. The standing demonstrators were excluded from that order. Plaintiff was never sitting, and thus was not included in the arrest order to the sitting demonstrators. Proof of this is that all the other standing demonstrators were blocking traffic, but were not arrested. Plaintiff's kidnapping was not part of a group arrest. It was a single isolated event.

Messrs. Cardozo and McCann argue that the relevant time to determine probable cause is when the arrest is ordered, not when the person is placed under arrest. No law nor court opinion is given to support this contention, and Plaintiff does not know of any. If any exists, it is void on its face.

When arrested, not many people would know if the arrest were legal, illegal, or that they were being kidnapped. They would not know until they consulted an attorney, assuming that the attorney knows. Even if they knew when arrested that it was illegal, how many old white men, or young black girls, would challenge 6 police officers, probably armed with guns and billy clubs? Plaintiff can name only one—himself.

In any event, Plaintiff challenged the "arrest" immediately when he was placed under "arrest" both times. It is certainly clear in the video that Plaintiff vociferously challenged the "arrest" order.

Messrs. Cardozo and McCann quote People v. Maher, 1137 Misc. 2d 162, 165 (N.Y. City Crim. Ct. 1987) "To be guilty of refusing a lawful order to disperse, a person must be congregating with others at the time the police order to disperse is ignored." Though this statement could not be found in the 3d Cir. Court Order in People v. Maher, Plaintiff agrees with this statement. He was not congregating with others.

In support of Plaintiff's contention that there was no cause for his arrest, he cites Cox v. Louisiana, 379 U. S. 536, 551 (1965). In that case Cox was arrested for:

> "[t]he inflammatory manner in which he [Cox] addressed that crowd and told them to go on up town, go to four places on the protest list, sit down and if they don't feed you, sit there for one hour." Cox was convicted on four counts. On appeal to the U. S. Supreme Court, the conviction was reversed because Court argued:
>
> "Our conclusion that the record does not support the contention that the students' cheering, clapping and singing

constituted a breach of the peace is confirmed by the fact that these were not relied on as a basis for conviction by the trial judge, who, Rather, stated as his reason for convicting Cox of disturbing the peace that:"

"[i]t must be recognized to be inherently dangerous and a breach of the peace to bring 1,500 people, colored people, down in the predominantly white business district in the City of Baton Rouge and congregate across the street from the courthouse and sing songs as described to me by the defendant as the CORE national anthem carrying lines such as 'black and white together' and to urge those 1,500 people to descend upon our lunch counters and sit there until they are served. That has to be an inherent breach of the peace, and our statute 14:103.1 has made it so."

The U. S. Supreme Court's finding was :

"A statute which, upon its face and as authoritatively construed, is so vague and indefinite as to permit the punishment of the fair use of this opportunity is repugnant to the guaranty of liberty contained in the Fourteenth Amendment."

"For all these reasons, we hold that appellant's freedoms of speech and assembly, secured to him by the First Amendment, as applied to the States by the Fourteenth Amendment, were denied by his conviction for disturbing the peace. The conviction on this charge cannot stand."

Certainly the police must know that, in view of this decision, a single man, standing alone on a public sidewalk without any body motions or saying anything at all cannot be obstructing traffic or disturbing the peace because he is holding signs. It is impossible to believe that police officers from a special task force for crowd control who were well prepared for this demonstration could be ignorant of this, especially since they had legal counsel with them at the demonstration.

A justified cause of arrest is for resisting arrest. However the resistance must occur before the arrest (e.g. The police approach someone and he runs away). Once the person is placed under arrest, any resistance by the arrestee (such as punching the police officer) cannot be a cause for arrest. The person was already under arrest. Of course, he can be charged with assault.

For some time now, Plaintiff has wondered how Mr. McCann graduated law school and passed a bar exam. Now Plaintiff wonders how either Messrs. Cardozo or McCann graduated high school.

Plaintiff understands that attorneys are paid to lie, but he expected some subtlety. Plaintiff's statement of the incident is Exhibit B. It was written on April 18, 2007, immediately after Plaintiff returned home from the arraignment. It was updated at 4:55 pm on April 19, 2007, immediately after Plaintiff returned home from measuring distances at the incident site. It still contains original typographical errors.

POINT IV: PLAINTIFF FAILS TO DISPUTE THAT OFFICER TOALA IS ENTITLED TO QUALIFIED IMMUNITY

Messrs. Cardozo and McCann told the truth again. They are on a run. However, it is not Plaintiff's responsibility to dispute that Officer Toala is entitled to qualified immunity. It is incumbent on Defendant to prove that he is entitled to immunity beyond any possible doubt (not reasonable doubt). It is not the responsibility of the moved party (Plaintiff) to dispute anything. The moving party (Defendants) must prove that Defendant Toala has qualified immunity beyond any doubt. Close to doubt does not prevail

[Anderson v. Creighton, 483 U.S. 635 at 644 (1987); Jenkins v. City of New York, 478 F.3d at 87, 2d Cir. (2007)].

Plaintiff supports police immunity when it is applicable. Plaintiff was involved in a case in which he supported police immunity. In 2005, the annual state governors' conference was held at Penn State University in State College, PA, where Plaintiff is an emeritus professor of chemistry. The conference held a dinner meeting one night in the Hetzel Union Building.

Across the street was the Osmond Laboratory of Physics. It was locked at 5:00 pm, and everyone was denied permission to enter. However before the building was locked a group of five students entered the building. Plaintiff was their faculty advisor. They went onto a balcony facing the Hetzel Union Building with protest signs.

The police entered the building and told the students to leave. The students told the police that they had permission to be there, but they had no written proof. The police arrested them for trespassing. They were carried away and committed at arraignment.

At the preliminary hearing, the University official responsible for buildings admitted that he gave the students verbal permission to occupy the building during the time of arrest. The district magistrate officiating at the preliminary hearing dismissed the case against the students. The students wanted to sue the police. Plaintiff and their attorney convinced them not to do this, because the police acted reasonably with the information at their disposal, and were entitled to immunity.

The present case does not meet that standard. Defendants argue that Officer Toala is entitled to qualified immunity, because officers of reasonable competence could have decided that there was probable cause for arrest. This is equivalent to letting the chickens guard the fox.

For a moving party to get a judgment during discovery, it must prove its case beyond any doubt. Asserting it is not proof. The moved party does not have to prove anything. In support of their assertion, the Defendants quote Zellner v. Summerlin, 494 F. 3d 344, 369 (2nd Cir. 2007). In Zellner v. Summerlin, a truck tried to enter a driveway and was blocked temporarily by Zellner. Zellner was arrested and charged with disorderly conduct. Later all charges were dropped.

Zellner sued the police in the U. S. District Court of Eastern New York for false arrest, malicious prosecution, and use of excessive force. The jury found in favor of Zellner and awarded him and his codefendant compensatory damages of $80,000 plus attorney costs plus punitive damages of $5500.

The police challenged the jury decision as a matter of law. The District Court judge ruled that the police were entitled to qualified immunity on the grounds that their behavior was reasonable based on the situation. A new final decision was made by the District Court judge to dismiss all of Zellner's claims.

Zellner appealed to the U. S. Court of Appeals for the 2nd Circuit. The Court of Appeals found the District Court to be in error on probable cause, but upheld the decision in regard to excessive force. The Court of Appeals concluded that "Zellner is also entitled to recover costs, including reasonable attorney fees, in connection with the portion of this appeal as to which he is the prevailing party. The amount is to be determined by the district court."

This case is interesting for three reasons:

Reason 1

This case was sited by Cardozo and McCann to show that the police were entitled to immunity. The Court of Appeals decided that the police are not entitled to immunity for violation of First

Amendment rights, thus disproving Defendants' claim. (How dumb can Cardozo and McCann get?)

Reason 2

It is distressing that the District Court judge overturned the jury's decision. If the trial judge can overrule a jury, what is the point of having a jury trial? The jury has the duty to judge the law as well as the facts.

This decision of the District Court judge to overrule the jury's decision shows the Court's contempt of the jury system. It also illustrates that the courts are in collusion with the police to protect them in their criminal activities. If this becomes common it is the end of constitutional government. That District Court judge should be removed from the judiciary.

Reason 3

The Court of Appeals Opinion discussed some critical issues. The District Court Judge stated: "If this occurred and the jury finds that it occurred the way the plaintiff says it occurred, there is no immunity. It is the law, because the factual dispute here, the factual dispute has to be resolved before there can be a finding of whether or not there is qualified immunity."

The court explained, *inter alia*, that "probable cause exists when the facts and circumstances within the knowledge of the police officers at the time the arrest was made were sufficient to warrant a person of reasonable prudence to believe that a violation or a crime has been committed by the person arrested." In his charge to the jury, the District Court Judge stated:

> "The arrest at issue must have been made...on probable cause. Also, resisting arrest does not accordance with the law. Namely, that it was based require that the person being arrested use force or violence. It is enough if he engages in

> his conduct with the intent of preventing the officer from effecting the authorized arrest of himself. Accordingly, on the issue of the alleged Constitutional violation, making an unlawful arrest for disorderly conduct or resisting arrest, if you determine that there was no probable cause to arrest plaintiff on either of those charges [and that defendants' actions were a proximate cause of injury to Zellner], your verdict will be in favor of the plaintiff and against the defendants, as to the Federal Section 1983 false arrest cause of action. However, if you determine that . . . there was probable cause to arrest plaintiff for either disorderly conduct or resisting arrest, then the arrest would be lawful and your verdict must be in favor of the defendants with regard to the charge of false arrest."

The Court of Appeals further stated that: "Once the jury has resolved any disputed facts that are material to the qualified immunity issue, the ultimate determination of whether the officer's conduct was objectively reasonable is to be made by the court." The Court further stated that:

> "Qualified immunity is an affirmative defense. See Gomez v. Toledo, 446 U.S. 635, 640 (1980). [B]ecause qualified immunity is an affirmative defense, it is incumbent upon the defendant to plead, and adequately develop, a qualified immunity defense during pretrial proceedings so that the trial court can determine . . . which facts material to the qualified immunity defense must be presented to the jury to determine its applicability once the case has gone to trial. Blissett v. Coughlin, 66 F.3d 531, 538 (2d Cir. 1995) (emphasis added). To the extent that a particular finding of fact is essential to a determination by the court that the defendant is entitled to qualified immunity, it is the

responsibility of the defendant to request that the jury be asked the pertinent question. See, *e.g., id.* If the defendant does not make such a request, he is not entitled to have the court, in lieu of the jury, make the needed factual finding. See, e.g., Kerman, 374 F.3d at 120; see also Warren, 906 F.2d at 76 ('the jury should decide these issues on special interrogatories') quoting Anderson v. Creighton, 483 U.S. at 641)."

"'Arguable probable cause' must 'not be misunderstood to mean "almost" probable cause.' (Jenkins v. City of New York, 478 F.3d 76, 87 (2d Cir. 2007). The essential inquiry in determining whether qualified immunity is available to an officer accused of false arrest is whether it was objectively reasonable for the officer to conclude that probable cause existed. See Anderson[v. Creighton], 483 U.S. at 644 . . . There should be no doubt that probable cause remains the relevant standard. If officers of reasonable competence would have to agree that the information possessed by the officer at the time of arrest did not add up to probable cause, the fact that it came close does not immunize the officer. Jenkins v. City of New York, 478 F.3d at (emphasis added)"

In summary close to probable cause does not immunize the officer. The question is who is to decide probable cause? Some Court decisions say that the Court should decide and some say that other police officers should decide. Plaintiff objects to both methods and prefers that the jury make the decision. To let other police officers make the decision is absurd. They would always support their fellow officers (This is known among police as the blue wall of silence.)

Preferable to other police officers making the decision is to have the trial judge make the decision. However there is a difficulty here as shown in Zellner's case. The police and judges are in criminal collusion and cannot be trusted to make honest decisions. The best solution, in Plaintiff's view, is to have an impartial jury make the decision.

Zellner further states:

"Thus a court may grant a motion for judgment as a matter of law 'only if it can conclude that, with credibility assessments made against the moving party, a reasonable juror would have been compelled to accept the view of the moving party.'"

"The Standard for Judgment as a Matter of Law In considering a motion for judgment as a matter of law, the district court must draw all reasonable inferences in favor of the nonmoving party, and it may not make credibility determinations or weigh the evidence. . . ." "Credibility determinations, the weighing of the evidence, and the drawing of legitimate inferences from the facts are jury functions, not those of a judge." . . . "Thus, although the court should review the record as a whole, it must disregard all evidence favorable to the moving party that the jury is not required to believe. Reeves v. Sanderson Plumbing, 530 U.S. 133, 150-51 (2000) (quoting Anderson v. Liberty Lobby, Inc., 477 U.S. 242, 255 (1986)) (emphases ours)."

"Thus, a court may grant a motion for judgment as a matter of law 'only if it can conclude that, with credibility assessments made against the moving party and all inferences drawn against the moving party, a reasonable juror would have been compelled to accept the view of the moving party.' Piesco v. Koch, 12 F.3d 332, 343 (2d Cir. 1993) (emphasis added). In ruling on a such motion, the court must bear in mind that the jury is free to believe part and disbelieve part of any witness's testimony. See, e.g., Fiacco v. City of Rensselaer, 783 F.2d 319, 325 (2d Cir. 1986), cert. denied, 480 U.S. 922 (1987); see also Haywood v. Koehler, 78 F.3d 101, 105 (2d Cir. 1996) (jurors are 'free to accept bits of testimony from several witnesses and to make reasonable inferences from whatever testimony they credit'). Incontrovertible evidence relied on by the moving party, such as a relevant videotape whose accuracy is unchallenged, should be credited by the court on such a motion if it so utterly discredits the opposing party's version that no reasonable juror could fail to believe the version advanced by the moving party. See Scott v. Harris, 127 S. Ct. 1769, 1775-76 (2007) (so holding with respect to proceedings on summary judgment); see generally Reeves, 530 U.S. at 150 ("the standard for granting summary judgment 'mirrors' the standard for judgment as a matter of law, such that 'the inquiry under each is the same'" (quoting Anderson v. Liberty Lobby, Inc., 477 U.S. at 250-51))."

"The court is not permitted to find as a fact a proposition that is contrary to a finding made by the jury. See, e.g., Smith v. Lightning Bolt Productions, Inc., 861 F.2d 363, 367 (2d Cir. 1988) (court 'cannot . . .substitute its judgment for that of the jury' (internal quotation marks omitted)); see also Leblanc-Sternberg v. Fletcher, 67 F. 3d 412, 430 (2d Cir. 1995) ('In ruling on the motion by [one codefendant] for judgment as a matter of law, . . . the court was required to view the evidence in the light most favorable to the [individual] plaintiffs; whatever its own view of the facts may have been, the court was not entitled to substitute its view for adequately supported findings that were implicit in the jury's verdict' against another defendant cert. denied, 518 U.S. 1017 (1996). Nor is the court permitted to make findings on factual questions not submitted to the jury where those findings take the evidence in the light most favorable to the moving party, rather than the opposing party. See, e.g., Kerman, 374 F.3d at 120."

Later Zellner further states:

"4. The Record in the Present Case. In the present case, defendants seek to defend the district court's decision granting them qualified immunity as a matter of law by asserting that they had actual or arguable probable cause to arrest Zellner (a) for disorderly conduct in violation of N.Y. Penal Law § 240.20(5), as charged, and (b) for other violations not charged, to wit, disorderly conduct in violation of subsections (6) and (7) of § 240.20 and obstructing the troopers' functioning in violation of Penal Law §195.05. We conclude, applying the above principles. that the record does not support qualified immunity on any of these bases."

CONCLUSION

Defendants' motion for summary judgment and damages must be denied for the following reasons:

a. Their Memorandum of law is a tissue of lies and misinterpretations of court decisions.
b. For dismissal the moving party must prove its case beyond any doubt. It has not done so.
c. The moved party does not have to prove anything.
d. If there is any uncertainty in the facts, they must be decided by the jury. The Court is prohibited from making this decision.
e. The Court cannot rule favorably on movant's motion until the facts are decided.
f. In any event, Judge Koeltl cannot make a decision, because he already has shown favoritism to Defendants and prejudice against Plaintiff. Plaintiff has filed **COMPLAINTS OF JUDICIAL MISCONDUCT** against Judge Koeltl with the U. S. Court of Appeals: Second Circuit and the Committee on Professional Ethics of the New York State Bar Association. Also he has filed criminal charges against Judge Koeltl with the U. S. Attorney. Judge Koeltl cannot make an unbiased decision.

I submitted the above document with a cover letter of November 9, 2009, which read:

"I have received Mr. McCann's correspondence of October 28, 2009. In his **DECLARATION OF MAX MCCANN IN OPPOSITION TO PLAINTIFF'S MOTION FOR DISCOVERY AND SUMMARY JUDGMENT**, McCann states in point 3 that he has not tampered with the sound track of the video. He may not have, but someone did, probably the police. He submitted tampered evidence."

"In Point 4, he claims to have acted in good faith. That may be his idea of good faith, because after all, he is a lawyer. This is the way lawyers act routinely. I doubt that any non-attorney would agree with him."

"In point 5 he claims that criminal proceedings against plaintiff are still pending. This may be a delusion of the district attorney, but it is just not so for the reasons given in my previous correspondence."

"I am not responding to Mr. McCann's and Cardozo's **MEMORANDUM OF LAW IN OPPOSITION TO PLAINTIFF'S MOTION FOR DISCOVERY AND SUMMARY JUDGMENT**, because it is just a rehash of previous lies. It is nothing but an attempt to waste time. I stand by my previous comprehensive submissions."

"Your behavior in this case has been atrocious. Your failure to recuse yourself just adds to your shamefulness and disregard for the law and decency."

"I am asking you again to recuse yourself from this case. Do not return this letter. Add it to the case record. If there is a rule against this, ignore the rule."

XXVI. COMPLAINT OF JUDICIAL MISCONDUCT

On December 28, 2009, I filed a complaint of Judicial Misconduct against Judge Koeltl to the Judicial Council of the **UNITED STATES COURT OF APPEALS: SECOND CIRCUIT** [Circuit Court Case # 08 4931-op, District Court Case # 08 CIV. 2457 (JGK)]. The Complaint contained the following:

A. OFFENSES OF THE JUDGE

I accused Judge Koeltl of obstruction of justice, because he violated his oath of office (28 U.S.C. §453) by doing the following:

a. refused to order Defendants to provide the identities of the John Doe Defendants. Three times Plaintiff submitted interrogatories to the Defense to produce the names of the John Doe police officers shown in the video introduced as evidence. All three requests were ignored. Three times Plaintiff moved that the Court order Defendants to comply. The first motion was denied. The second and third motions were ignored.
b. applied the rules of Court differently to the Plaintiff and Defendants.
c. failed to render judgment against Defendant Toala, who did not respond to the summons in a timely fashion.
d. accepted documents from the Defense which were not prepared in accordance with the rules of the Court.
e. ordered Plaintiff to produce information which does not exist.
f. delayed the progress of the trial by considering ridiculous claims of the Defendants.
g. Defendants Kelly and Toala were served on March 2, 2009. Many informations and Memoranda of Law have been

transmitted, but this case has not moved one inch forward from March 2, 2009.

Disciplinary action is authorized by **RULES FOR JUDICIAL-CONDUCT AND JUDICIAL- DISABILITY PROCEEDINGS.**

B. CHARGES

Judge Koeltl is charged with:

a. obstruction of justice.
b. failure to apply Court rules impartially.
c. delaying proceedings for no justifiable reasons.
d. ordering Plaintiff to supply information that does not exist.
e. Conspiracy against rights in violation of 18 U.S.C. Ch. 13 #241 and #242

C. REMEDIES SOUGHT

a. Recusal of Judge Koeltl from trying this case.
b. Appointment of another Judge to continue the trial.

XXVII. DECISION ON JUDICIAL MISCONDUCT

On March 1, 2010 Dennis Jacobs the Chief Judge of the U. S. Court of Appeals: Second Circuit dismissed my complaint, because Judge Koeltl may have made wrong decisions, but this not judicial misconduct. I replied in a **PETITION FOR REVIEW** on March 24, 2010, as follows:

A. CIRCUIT COURT OPINION

The U. S. Court of Appeals: Second Circuit Chief Judge dismissed the complaint because "the vast majority of alleged allegations in the complaint merely attack the correctness of the Judge's various rulings and official actions."

It is not the correctness of the rulings that Petitioner is attacking, but the fact that the judge rules differently for each party. For example, the judge ordered Plaintiff to provide discovery, but refuses to order Defendants to supply discovery, even though the judge has stated that the Defendants are obligated to do so.

The dismissal also states that "The allegations of bias and conspiracy are wholly unsupported."

The dismissal also states that "The Petitioner next moved to "close the pleadings" for some Defendants, because those Defendants had not answered the complaint. The Judge denied the motion, explaining that he had previously extended the Defendants."

The above two statements have nothing to do with each other. The court rules state that a Defendant must respond to a summons within 30 days or judgment **WILL** (not may) be rendered against the Defendant. Defendant Toala never responded. Attorney McCann made an appearance for him on July 17, 2009, 3-1/2 months after the summons was received (March 2, 2009).

B. JUDGE KOELTL'S RULING

Since Plaintiff's complaint was submitted to the Circuit Court, Judge Koeltl has rendered a decision in favor of Defendants and dismissed the case. In Judge Koeltl's Memorandum, he states that summary judgment may not be granted unless "the pleadings, the discovery and discovery materials on file, and any affidavits show that there is no genuine issue as to any material fact and that the movant is entitled to judgment as a matter of law."

Judge Koeltl also states that "only disputed facts that might affect the outcome of the suit under the governing law will properly preclude the entry of a summary judgment." He further states that: "A court may determine that there is no genuine dispute as to certain facts when one party's version of the facts is 'blatantly contradicted by the video evidence.'" Judge Koeltl states that the Plaintiff "offers no evidence showing that the video has been altered." This is a blatant lie.

Judge Koeltl further states "Defendant Toala has qualified immunity in this case." Another lie. However Judge Koeltl states that immunity only applies if "their conduct does not violate clearly established statutory or constitutional rights of which a reasonable person would have known."

Judge Koeltl dismissed the complaint for two reasons:

a. The video shows incontrovertible evidence that the arrest was justified.
b. The police have immunity.

C. PETITIONER'S REBUTTAL

Petitioner's rebuttal occurs in two documents submitted to the District Court. These are Letter of Plaintiff to Judge Koeltl of

August 18, 2009, and Memorandum of Law of October 18, 2009. Both are enclosed.

The Memorandum of Law contains the video time line which shows that at:

0:06 Police blue shield appears.
0:25 Lieutenant Wolf announces that he is on the bullhorn.
0:40 Demonstrators ordered to clear the steps and sidewalk or be arrested.
0:50 Plaintiff is seen standing behind the sitting demonstrators.
1:38 Another picture of Plaintiff standing behind the sitting demonstrators.
2:25 Picture of standing demonstrators with pedestrians moving by unobstructed.
2:43 The sitting demonstrators ordered to leave the staircase or be arrested for disorderly conduct. Plaintiff is not in the picture.
2:53 Plaintiff is shown standing behind the sitting demonstrators who are ordered to leave or be arrested. Nobody has been arrested yet.
3:05 Plaintiff is shown standing at the head of the standing demonstrators.
3:19 & 3:37: Pedestrians are escorted by the police through the sitting demonstrators.
3:45 First sitting demonstrators taken into custody.
4:05 Plaintiff is not in the picture.
4:22 Plaintiff is not among the sitting demonstrators.
5:07 Warning that if you do not want to be arrested, clear the stairs now. Plaintiff is not in the picture.
5:14 Warning is given by police that all sitting demonstrators will be arrested.

6:29 Warning that remaining sitting demonstrators must clear the steps now or be arrested also.
7:22 Plaintiff is shown standing alone well behind the sitting demonstrators. A police officer is standing right behind the sitting demonstrators.
7:28 There is a full shot of the Plaintiff holding signs, but not making body movement or saying anything. Pedestrian traffic is not blocked.
7:34 A pedestrian walks by Plaintiff unimpeded.
7:54 There is a free flow of pedestrian traffic through the last several sitting demonstrators.
9:06 There is shot of the last 6 sitting demonstrators. Plaintiff is not in the picture.
11:00 Last sitting demonstrator is removed.
11:10 Sidewalk and stairs are cleared. Pedestrians walk by.
11:19 Police Approach standing Plaintiff.
11:25 There is conversation between the police officer and Plaintiff that is not audible (presumably deleted from the video).
11:33 Another police officer joins the first police officer and Plaintiff.
11:39 Plaintiff falls down for no apparent reason (sound has been deleted from the video).
11:47 A woman approaches Plaintiff (who identified herself as a nurse, but this statement is not on the video).
11:50 A pedestrian easily passes Plaintiff, who is still on the ground motionless.
11:56 Five police officers (one in plain clothes) around Plaintiff. One says to call 911.
12:00 Another police officer approaches.
12:06 The plain clothes officer leaves.
12:31 Police call for a carry detail.

12:41 Nurse asks the police why Plaintiff is being arrested. It appears that Plaintiff is unconscious.
12:50 There are about 5 police officers near Plaintiff. The sound track is muffled.
13:24 Plaintiff starts to rise.
13:38 There is a muffled conversation.
13:49 Plaintiff informs police that he has a permit to be there.
14:03 Plaintiff reads Amendment I from his pocket U. S. Constitution.
14:30 Plaintiff warns police that if arrested, they will be sued.
14:36 Plaintiff lies down again.
14:44 Plaintiff voices vociferous objection.
14:48 Police start dragging Plaintiff away.
14:54 Officer says that Plaintiff should be charged with resisting arrest.
16:00 Six police officers carry Plaintiff away.
16:25 A police officer announces that the time is 13:05 (1:05 pm).
17:08 Officer Rivera announce that the demonstration is concluded.

It should be notice that:

0:40 Demonstrators ordered to clear the steps and sidewalk or be arrested.
0:50 Plaintiff is seen standing behind the sitting demonstrators.
2:43 The sitting demonstrators ordered to leave the staircase or be arrested for disorderly conduct. Plaintiff is not in the picture. Nor was he sitting or on the steps.
2:53 Plaintiff is shown standing behind the sitting demonstrators who are ordered to leave or be arrested. Nobody has been arrested yet. The Plaintiff was never

sitting or on the steps at any time. Arrest order does not apply to Plaintiff.

5:07 Warning that if you do not want to be arrested, clear the stairs now. Plaintiff is not in the picture.

5:14 Warning is given by police that all sitting demonstrators will be arrested.

6:29 Warning that remaining sitting demonstrators must clear the steps now or be arrested also.

7:22 Plaintiff is shown standing alone well behind the sitting demonstrators. A police officer is standing right behind the sitting demonstrators.

7:28 There is a full shot of the Plaintiff holding signs, but not making body movement or saying anything. Pedestrian traffic is not blocked.

7:34 A pedestrian walks by Plaintiff unimpeded.

11:50 A pedestrian easily passes Plaintiff, who is still on the ground motionless.

After all the sitting demonstrators were arrested the police approached Plaintiff and ordered him to move back with the other demonstrators or be arrested. Plaintiff is not under arrest at this point. Plaintiff refuses and gets arrested. This part of the video has been deleted.

It should be noticed that the video shows:

a. Plaintiff was never sitting nor on the stairs.
b. Only sitting demonstrators were arrested.
c. No other standing demonstrators were arrested even though they were congregated, singing, using electronic equipment and rams' horns, holding signs, as well as blocking pedestrian traffic.

d. Plaintiff was not blocking any traffic. In only one scene was a pedestrian passing Plaintiff, and that was without any difficulty.
e. Plaintiff was never placed under arrest in the video. That part has been deleted from the video.
f. Plaintiff was "arrested" after all the sitting demonstrators had been removed.
g. The police did not approach Plaintiff until 11:19 above.

The arrest deposition is shown as Item 7 and Exhibit A in the Memorandum of Law. Let us examine the reasons given for arrest in the deposition.

a. "Deponent observed the Defendant lying/sitting on the floor at the above location on the steps and sidewalk." This does not occur in the video until after police officers apprehended Plaintiff. Plaintiff was never on the steps.
b. "blocking the normal flow of pedestrian traffic and obstructing pedestrian traffic as follows: pedestrians had to walk around the Defendant and pedestrians were unable to access stairs and access to the above location." This never occurs anywhere in the video. It is an outright lie.
c. Defendant's conduct created a public disturbance/ inconvenience in that it caused a crowd to gather, disruption of the normal flow of traffic, and people to express alarm." None of this occurs in the video when Plaintiff is standing alone. It only happens after he is accosted and surrounded by police. The police caused the public disturbance, and are the ones who should have been arrested.
d. "Deponent further states that when he was placing the Defendant under arrest for the offense(s) describe above Defendant (sic) the Defendant laid on the steps and

refused to stand up and place Defendant's hands behind Defendant's back." Even if this were true, it cannot be a cause for arrest, since it would have happened after Plaintiff was placed under arrest.

There are many conflicts between the video and Police Officer Toala's deposition.

a. Deponent Toala states that he placed the Plaintiff under arrest (not detention) for several listed crimes by Plaintiff at or about 12:51 hours.
b. At 16:25 on the tape, a police officer announces the time to be 1:05 pm.
c. Thus Plaintiff was placed under "arrest" 14 minutes earlier, or at 2:25 on the tape time. There is no possibility of this being true since none of the sitting demonstrators has been taken into custody at this time.
d. Either Deponent Toala is mistaken (lying) or a significant part of the tape is missing.
e. It would not be surprising if Deponent Toala is lying, since every other allegation in the deposition disagrees with the video evidence. However there seems to be no logical reason for Deponent Toala to lie about the time of "arrest."
f. We must conclude that part of the video is missing. Petitioner can provide witnesses to testify to this.

D. ALLOWABLE GROUNDS FOR DISMISSAL

RULES FOR JUDICIAL-CONDUCT AND JUDICIAL-DISABILITY PROCEEDINGS for the 2nd Circuit Rule 11(c) (1) Allowable grounds. A complaint must be dismissed in whole or in part to the extent that the chief judge concludes that the complaint:

A) alleges conduct that, even if true, is not prejudicial to the effective and expeditious administration of the business of the courts and does not indicate a mental or physical disability resulting in inability to discharge the duties of judicial office;"

The conduct is prejudicial to the effective and expeditious administration of the business of the courts, which is to try cases impartially and on their merits. It does indicate a mental disability — the inability to understand the English language.

B) is directly related to the merits of a decision or procedural ruling;"

Discrepancies in several rulings are mentioned. Dismissal of the case without a trial is hardly a procedural ruling. Furthermore the allegation is not based only on discrepancy in rulings, but because the judge is mentally incompetent to understand the English language and is in collusion with the police to obstruct justice.

C) is frivolous;"

The complaint is not frivolous because Plaintiff was not allowed to have a trial.

D) is based on allegations lacking sufficient evidence to raise an inference that misconduct has occurred or that a disability exists;"

The evidence is that the judge claimed irrefutable evidence when the two pieces of evidence were in direct conflict. He also claimed that police Defendant Toala has immunity in direct conflict with U. S. Supreme Court decisions. Furthermore the Judge ordered Plaintiff to produce discovery material, but refused to order Defendants to do so, even though the judge stated at least twice that Defendants were obligated to provide this information.

E) is based on allegations which are incapable of being established through investigation;"

Plaintiff certainly can establish the allegations if he can question witnesses. Furthermore, he has already established that Deponent Toala committed perjury, and that the Defendants have submitted a tampered DVD video.

F) has been filed in the wrong circuit under Rule 7;"

Not applicable.

G) is otherwise not appropriate for consideration under the Act."

Not applicable.

E. CLAIMS

The Defendants have two pieces of evidence —the DVD video and the arrest deposition. They are in complete conflict with each other. Yet Judge Koeltl claims that they provide irrefutable evidence. Judge Koeltl does not understand English. Judge Koeltl is mentally incompetent. Judge Koeltl does not adhere to U. S. Supreme Court decisions regarding police immunity. Judge Koeltl is in criminal collusion with the Defendants to obstruct justice.

F. REMEDIES

The case should be returned to the District Court for trial. Judge Koeltl should be recused and replaced with an honest, mentally competent Judge who understands English and follows Supreme Court rulings. Judge Koeltl should be removed from the bench and criminally prosecuted.

The new District judge should order Defendants to respond to Plaintiff's interrogatories. The new District judge should be ordered to submit a schedule for a speedy jury trial. The schedule should include dates for responses to interrogatories, interviewing witnesses before trial, establishing jury selection procedures, convening a jury pool, selecting a jury, and setting a trial date.

The Clerk of Court and *Pro Se* Clerk of the District Court should be ordered to respond promptly to Plaintiff's request for information.

Petitioner demands a jury trial as required by Amendment VII of the U. S. Constitution.

XXVIII. JUDGMENT FOR DISMISSAL

On February 17, 2010, Judge Koeltl issued a **MEMORANDUM OPINION AND ORDER** for summary judgment against me on the grounds "that the pleadings, the discovery and disclosure materials on file, and any affidavits show that there is no genuine issue as to any material fact and that the movant is entitled to judgment as a matter of law."

Judge Koeltl also referred to court cases to state that: "Summary judgment is improper if there is any evidence in the record from any source from which a reasonable inference could be drawn in favor of the non-moving party. See Chambers v. T. R. M. Copy Ctrs. Corp., 43 F.3d 29, 37 (2d Cir. 1994)." Judge Koeltl also states: "At the summary judgment stage, facts must be viewed in the light most favorable to the nonmoving party only if there is 'genuine' dispute as those facts. Scott v. Harris, 550 U. S. 372, 380 (2007). A court may determine that there is no genuine dispute as to certain facts when one party's version of the facts is 'blatantly contradicted' by video evidence. Id. at 379–81."

Apparantly the fact that the video never showed me being placed under arrest and was tampered evidence in direct conflict with Police Officer Toala's deposition did not influence Judge Koeltl.

On February 22, 2010, J. Michael McMahon, Clerk of Court, issued a **JUDGMENT** for dismissal and Bill of Costs. Judge Koeltl "**ORDERED, ADJUDGED AND DECREED**: That for the reasons given in the Court's Opinion and Order dated Februry 17, 2010, defendants Kelly and Toala's motion for summary judgment dismissing the plaintiff's complaint is granted; plaintiff's motion for summary judgment is denied; defendants motion to stay discovery and the plaintiff's motion to compel discovery are denied as moot: plaintiff's motion for a default judgment against defendant Toala and the plaintiff's motion for contempt against defense counsel are denied; and judgment is entered dismissing the amended complaint with prejudice except for any state law claim of conversion which is dismissed without prejudice, according, the case is closed, including all pending motions.

XXIX. APPEAL OF THE DISMISSAL

On March 24, 2010, I filed a **NOTICE OF APPEAL** which stated:

1. This appeal is being filed in accordance with **CIRCUIT COURT APPELLATE PROCEDURE** Rule 3 (c):

   Rule 3(c)(1)(A): Appellant is Julian Heicklen, Plaintiff. Appellees are the Defendants and their counsels, Max McCann and Michael A. Cardozo

   Rule 3(c)(1)(B): The whole case is being appealed. Specifically the **MEMORANDUM OPINION AND ORDER** of Judge John G. Koeltl of February 17, 2010, is being appealed.

   Rule 3(c)(1)(C)): The appeal is being taken to the U. S. Court of Appeals for the Second Circuit.

2. This is an appeal of right under Rules 4(a)(1)(A)

3. The District Court is requested to forward the reproduced record and a certified copy of the docket entries to the U. S. Court of Appeals for the Second Circuit as required under Circuit Court Appellate Procedure: the Record of Procedure Rules 10(a)(1), and 10(a)(3).

4. No transcript will be ordered in accordance with Rule 10(b)(1)(B).

6. Enclosed is the filing fee of $455.00.

7. Petitioner moves that the Court of Appeals nullify the **ORDER** of Judge Koeltl of February 17, 2010.

8. Plaintiff further moves that the case be remanded to the District Court for **TRIAL BY JURY** as required by Amendment VII of the U. S. Constitution.

9. Plaintiff additionally moves that Judge Koeltl must be recused and replaced by a Judge who will uphold the law.

XXX. APPELLANT'S SUPPORT OF APPEAL

On July 2, 2010, I filed my brief in support of the appeal.

ABSTRACT

Judge Koeltl dismissed this case and rendered judgment on behalf of Defendants for three reasons:

1. Police Officer Toala has immunity from prosecution because he was performing his duty.
2. Commissioner Kelly has immunity because he is the *respondiat superior*.
3. Plaintiff has no case because the video shows irrefutable evidence of his guilt.

Plaintiff argues:

1. Police Officer Toala made an illegal seizure in violation of Amendment I of the U. S. constitution. He was made aware by Plaintiff that he was in violation. When asked the reason for arrest, the only reason given at the scene was "Failure to obey an order of a police officer." This is not a legitimate reason for arrest. It has been deleted from the video.
2. Plaintiff alleges that Commissioner Kelly orchestrated, or at least was aware of, the police action and was involved in planning and effecting it. He even had a legal advisor and several senior officers from a special task force execute his orders. Thus he is not immune under *respondiat superior*.
3. The video does not show irrefutable evidence of Plaintiff's guilt. Nowhere in the video is Plaintiff placed under arrest.

Actually Plaintiff was placed under arrest twice. That part of the video was deleted by the police. In some part of the video, the sound has been muffled. The video shows that Plaintiff was the last person taken into custody. The time of arrest on the police deposition indicates that Plaintiff was the first person taken into custody. Both statements cannot be true.

4. Plaintiff intends to produce witnesses that can corroborate his statements, if given the opportunity.

A. HISTORY

The sequence of events for filing the **NOTICE OF APPEAL** was:

a. The District Court **JUDGMENT** and **ORDER OF DISMISSAL** was signed by Judge Koeltl on February 22, 2010.

b. It was mailed to the Plaintiff by the District Court on March 4, 2010.

c. Appellant mailed the **NOTICE OF APPEAL** to the District Court on March 10, 2010.

d. Because it was incomplete, the *Pro Se* Clerk returned it to Plaintiff on March 16, 2010.

e. A revised NOTICE OF APPEAL was mailed on March 24, 2010.

f. On March 30, 2010, the *Pro Se* Clerk notified Plaintiff that it was received on March 26, 2010.

Appellant received the **DOCKETING NOTICE** dated April 12, 2010 from the U. S. Court of Appeals, which contained the case docket #10–1251. Appellant mailed the Acknowledgment and Notice of Appearance form immediately upon receipt. There is no date on the form. The due date for the Brief of Appellant has not been specified by the Court of Appeals. The appeal is from the

JUDGMENT and **ORDER OF DISMISSAL** issued on February 22, 2010, by Judge Koeltl of the U. S. District Court.

B. THE ISSUES

Appellant sued Defendants under 42 U.S.C. §1983 for damages for deprivation of rights. Statute 42 U.S.C. §1983 reads:

> "Every person who, under color of any statute, ordinance, regulation, custom, or usage, of any State or Territory or the District of Columbia, subjects, or causes to be subjected, any citizen of the United States or other person within the jurisdiction thereof to the deprivation of any rights, privileges, or immunities secured by the Constitution and laws, shall be liable to the party injured in an action at law, suit in equity, or other proper proceeding for redress, except that in any action brought against a judicial officer for an act or omission taken in such officer's judicial capacity, injunctive relief shall not be granted unless a declaratory decree was violated or declaratory relief was unavailable. For the purposes of this section, any Act of Congress applicable exclusively to the District of Columbia shall be considered to be a statute of the District of Columbia."

Judge Koeltl dismissed the claim and awarded expenses of $123.56 to defendants based on two issues (Koeltl **Order & Judgment** of 2/22/10):

a. The DVD video shows irrefutable evidence that the police committed no violation
b. Police have immunity from prosecution.

C. DVD VIDEO DESCRIPTION OF EVENTS

The video timeline is:

Real Time, h:m	DVD Time, m:s	
	0:06	Police blue shield appears.
12:49	0:25	Lieutenant Wolf announces that he is on the bullhorn.
	0:40	Demonstrators ordered to clear the steps and sidewalk or be arrested.
	0:50	Plaintiff is seen standing behind the sitting demonstrators.
	1:38	Another picture of Plaintiff standing behind the sitting demonstrators.
12:51	2:25	Picture of standing demonstrators with pedestrians moving by unobstructed.
	2:43	The sitting demonstrators ordered to leave the staircase or be arrested for disorderly conduct. Plaintiff is not in the picture.
	2:53	Plaintiff is shown standing behind the sitting demonstrators who are ordered to leave or be arrested. Nobody has been arrested yet.
	3:05	Plaintiff is shown standing at the head of the standing demonstrators.
12:52	3:19 & 3:37:	Pedestrians are escorted by the police through the sitting demonstrators.
	3:45	First sitting demonstrators taken into custody.
	4:05	Plaintiff is not in the picture.
12:53	4:22	Plaintiff is not among the sitting demonstrators.

	5:07 Warning that if you do not want to be arrested, clear the stairs now. Plaintiff is not in the picture.
12:54	5:14 Warning is given by police that all sitting demonstrators will be arrested.
12:55	6:29 Warning that remaining sitting demonstrators must clear the steps now or be arrested also.
12:56	7:22 Plaintiff is shown standing alone well behind the sitting demonstrators. A police officer is standing right behind the sitting demonstrators.
	7:28 There is a full shot of the Plaintiff holding signs, but not making body movement or saying anything. Pedestrian traffic is not blocked.
	7:34 A pedestrian walks by Plaintiff unimpeded.
	7:54 There is a free flow of pedestrian traffic through the last sitting demonstrators.
12:58	9:06 There is shot of the last 6 sitting demonstrators. Plaintiff is not in the picture.
	11:00 Last sitting demonstrator is removed.
	11:10 Sidewalk and stairs are cleared. Pedestrians walk by.
	11:19 Police Approach standing Plaintiff.
13:00	11:25 There is conversation between the police officer and Plaintiff that is not audible (presumably deleted from the video).
	11:33 Another police officer joins the first police officer and Plaintiff.

11:39 Plaintiff falls down for no apparent reason (sound has been deleted from the video).

11:47 A woman approaches Plaintiff (who identified herself as a nurse, but this statement is not on the video).

11:50 A pedestrian easily passes Plaintiff, who is still on the ground motionless.

11:56 Five police officers (one in plain clothes) around Plaintiff. One says to call 911.

12:00 Another police officer approaches.

12:06 The plain clothes officer leaves.

13:01, 12:31 Police call for a carry detail.

12:41 Nurse asks the police why Plaintiff is being arrested. It appears that Plaintiff is unconscious.

12:50 There are about 5 police officers near Plaintiff. The sound track is muffled.

12:52, First sitting demonstrators taken into custody.

12:53–12:55: Warning that if you do not want to be arrested, clear the stairs now. Plaintiff is not in the picture. Warning is given by police that all sitting demonstrators will be arrested. Warning that remaining sitting demonstrators must clear the steps now or be arrested also.

12:56: Plaintiff is shown standing alone well behind the sitting demonstrators. A police officer is standing right behind the sitting demonstrators. There is a full shot of the Plaintiff holding signs, but not making body movement or saying anything. Pedestrian traffic is not blocked. A pedestrian walks by Plaintiff unimpeded.

12:59: Last sitting demonstrator is removed. Sidewalk and stairs are cleared. Pedestrians walk by.

13:00: There is conversation between the police officer and Plaintiff that is not audible (presumably deleted from the video) Another police officer joins the first police officer and Plaintiff. Plaintiff falls down for no apparent reason (sound has been deleted from the video). A woman approaches Plaintiff (who identified herself as a nurse, but this statement is not on the video).

13:01: Police call for a carry detail. Nurse asks the police why Plaintiff is being arrested. It appears that Plaintiff is unconscious. There are about 5 police officers near Plaintiff. The sound track is muffled.

13:03

13:38 There is a muffled conversation.

13:49 Plaintiff informs police that he has a permit to be there.

14:03 Plaintiff reads Amendment I from his pocket U. S. Constitution.

14:30 Plaintiff warns police that if arrested, they will be sued.

14:36 Plaintiff lies down again.

14:44 Plaintiff voices vociferous objection.

14:48 Police start dragging Plaintiff away.

14:54 Officer says that Plaintiff should be charged with resisting arrest.

16:00 Six police officers carry Plaintiff away.

13:05 16:25 A police officer announces that the time is 13:05 (1:05 pm)

17:08 Officer Rivera announce that the demonstration is concluded.

D. MISSING PART OF VIDEO

It is apparent that the video has been tampered, since part of the sound track is muffled. In addition a section has been deleted. The missing part is described in Plaintiff's description of events, written on the following day.

Several rabbis sat on the stairs and blocked the stairs. The other demonstrators were told to move back, and did so. Plaintiff moved back 13 feet, the others much farther back, so that there was a 22-foot separation between them and Plaintiff.

The rabbis were arrested one or two at a time. After their arrests, there was no one in front of Plaintiff for at least 40 feet or behind him for at least 22 feet. He was standing alone next to the chain railing 8 feet from the Isaiah wall. The police approached him and asked him to move back with the other demonstrators, 22 feet behind him. He refused saying that he was not bothering anyone.

The police repeated that he must move or be arrested. He insisted that he had the right to be there, and that an arrest could result in a law suit. The police then put Plaintiff under arrest and reached for him. He went limp. He fell to the ground and lay still and uttered no sound.

A woman approached Plaintiff, introduced herself as a nurse, and asked if he was alright. He did not answer at first. She pleaded with the police that he was an old man and that they should not arrest him. After some pleading the police agreed on the condition that Plaintiff would leave this location.

Plaintiff sat up, assured the woman that he was OK and stood up. He told the police that he would not leave, that he had a permit to be there. He read to the police officers Amendment I from his pocket U. S. Constitution.

The police said that Plaintiff would be arrested. He asked for what reason, and was told for refusing to obey the order of a law enforcement official. Plaintiff again went limp and fell to the ground.

From then until in his cell at the police station for some time, Plaintiff did not move a muscle or utter any sound. When on the ground, the police lifted and dragged Plaintiff to the police wagon, carried him into the wagon, and carried him into a cell at police headquarters. He was placed in a holding cell at police headquarters and did not move a muscle or utter any sound until approached by medics from the fire department.

As far as Plaintiff could tell, no-one except the police officers were anywhere in his vicinity at the time of the confrontation and arrest. He is unaware that anyone else was arrested together with him.

E. JUDGE KOELTL'S VERSION OF EVENTS IN ORDER OF 2/22/10

Judge Koeltl states: "A police officer using a loudspeaker (who identified himself as Lieutenant Wolf) ordered the group to leave the area and warned those who refused that they would be arrested." This order was directed only to the demonstrators sitting on the stairs and not to any of the standing demonstrators behind them. This was made clear by two subsequent announcements of the police at:

a. 12:54 5:14 Warning is given by police that all sitting demonstrators will be arrested.
b. 12:55 6:29 Warning that remaining sitting demonstrators must clear the steps now or be arrested also.

Judge Koeltl states: "After the warnings, some of those in the group behind the rabbis, including members of the group behind the plaintiff, moved back and left the area, but the plaintiff remained standing behind the seated rabbis." This statement of Judge Koeltl is false. Before the arrests, the standing demonstrators, including Plaintiff who was in the group (not in front of it), were moved back 35 feet by the police. They could not be seen from the street, so Plaintiff moved forward to 13 feet behind the rabbis. The other demonstrators did not leave the area. They remained, sang, blew rams' horns, used electronic equipment, and blocked pedestrian traffic. None of them were arrested.

Judge Koeltl states: "When the police reached the plaintiff to arrest him, he went limp and fell to the ground." This is an outright lie. The police did not approach plaintiff to arrest him, but to order him to move back with the other standing demonstrators (deleted from the video). Plaintiff refused on First Amendment grounds. The police then placed him under arrest (twice). When Plaintiff asked on what grounds, the only reason given was for failure to obey an order of the police. No mention was made of any of the other charges in the deposition. Plaintiff was the only standing demonstrator arrested, even though the others were congregated, causing a public nuisance, and blocking pedestrian traffic. Later in his memorandum, Judge Koeltl admits that plaintiff was not arrested until after approached by the police.

F. IRREFUTABLE EVIDENCE

Both the Judge and the Defendants claim that the video shows indisputable evidence. Plaintiff disagrees for the following reasons.

a. The video has been tampered as indicated by the fact that part of the sound has been muffled.
b. In addition part of the video is missing as described in Plaintiff's statement above.
c. Witnesses, especially the nurse, can confirm that part of the video is missing.
d. No place in the video is Plaintiff placed under arrest, yet he is dragged away by the police. Obviously, something is missing.
e. The police deposition by Defendant Toala states the time of arrest at 12:51 pm. According to the video timeline, this would make Plaintiff the first arrestee. However the video shows him to be the last arrestee.

G. POLICE IMMUNITY ACCORDING TO JUDGE KOELTL

Judge Koeltl states: "In analyzing §1983 claims for false arrest, courts in this circuit generally look to the law of the state in which the arrest occurred. Davis v. Rodriguez, 364 F.3d 424, 433 & n.7 (2nd Cir. 2004). In New York, probable cause is a complete defense to an action for false arrest. Burns v. City of New York, 791 N.Y.S.2d 851, 851 (App. Div. 2005). Probable cause exists if the arresting officer had "information sufficient to support a reasonable belief that an offense has been committed" by the person to be arrested. Id. at 852. In New York, a person is guilty of disorderly conduct when a person "congregates with other persons in a public place and refuses to comply with a lawful order of the police to disperse." N. Y. Penal Law.

The officers had no belief at all that an offense had been committed. Plaintiff was not congregating with other people. He was standing alone. None of the standing people who were congregating were arrested or even approached. Plaintiff was not arrested for failure to disperse, which would have been impossible, but for failure to obey an unlawful order of the police. Plaintiff asserted his First Amendment rights to peaceably protest and read the First Amendment of the U. S. Constitution to the police officers.

Judge Koeltl further states: "In this case, the police gave several orders for the plaintiff and others to disperse from the stairs and walkway in front of the Isaiah Wall. This statement is not true. The video shows an announcement at 5:07 video time: "Warning that if you do not want to be arrested, clear the stairs now." This announcement made it clear that the order did not apply to the standing demonstrators, and none of the other standing demonstrators were arrested.

Judge Koeltl further states that Lieutenant Wolf then advises the crowd that they are under arrest for refusing to leave the area. This is not true. At 2:43 video time, the sitting demonstrators were ordered to leave the staircase or be arrested for disorderly conduct. Plaintiff is not in the picture. Judge Koeltl admits this when he quotes the video at 5:00-5:13 "If you do not want to be arrested you are going to have to clear the stairs now. This is not going to wait until we get to you." Plaintiff was never on the stairs.

Subsequent announcements by the police made it clear that the order applied only to demonstrators sitting on the stairs. No standing demonstrator was ever threatened to be arrested for congregating, and none was. Plaintiff was not a congregant when place under arrest.

H. PLAINTIFF'S ARGUMENT FOR DENYING IMMUNITY

Several court decisions have stated that police do not have immunity if they know, or should have known, that no legal reason existed for their actions. (See Heicklen, **RESPONSE MEMORANDUM OF LAW TO REPLY MEMORANDUM OF LAW IN FURTHER SUPPORT OF DEFENDANTS' MOTION TO DISMISS OR, IN THE ALTERNATIVE, FOR SUMMARY JUDGMENT**, October 19, 2009.

It is not Plaintiff's responsibility to dispute that Officer Toala is entitled to qualified immunity. It is incumbent on Defendants to prove that he is entitled to immunity beyond any possible doubt (not reasonable doubt). It is not the responsibility of the moved party (Plaintiff) to dispute anything. The moving party (Defendants) must prove that Defendant Toala has qualified immunity beyond any doubt. Close to doubt does not prevail [Anderson v. Creighton, 483 U.S. 635 at 644 (1987); Jenkins v. City of New York, 478 F.3d at 87, 2d Cir. (2007)].

Defendants argue that Officer Toala is entitled to qualified immunity, because officers of reasonable competence could have decided that there was probable cause for arrest. This is equivalent to letting the chickens guard the fox.

For a moving party to get a judgment during discovery, it must prove its case beyond any doubt. Asserting it is not proof. The moved party does not have to prove anything.

In support of their assertion, the Defendants quote Zellner v. Summerlin, 494 F.3d 344, 369 (2nd Cir. 2007). In Zellner v. Summerlin, a truck tried to enter a driveway and was blocked temporarily by Zellner. Zellner was arrested and charged with disorderly conduct. Later all charges were dropped.

Zellner sued the police in the U. S. District Court of Eastern New York for false arrest, malicious prosecution, and use of excessive force. The jury found in favor of Zellner and awarded him and his codefendant compensatory damages of $80,000 plus attorney costs plus punitive damages of $5500.

The police challenged the jury decision as a matter of law. The District Court judge ruled that the police were entitled to qualified immunity on the grounds that their behavior was reasonable based on the situation. A new final decision was made by the District Court judge to dismiss all of Zellner's claims.

Zellner appealed to the U. S. Court of Appeals for the 2nd Circuit. The Court of Appeals found the District Court to be in error on probable cause, but upheld the decision in regard to excessive force. The Court of Appeals concluded that "Zellner is also entitled to recover costs, including reasonable attorney fees, in connection with the portion of this appeal as to which he is the prevailing party, the amount is to be determined by the district court."

This case is interesting for three reasons:

Reason 1

a. This case was sited by Cardozo and McCann to show that the police were entitled to immunity.
b. The Court of Appeals decided that the police are not entitled to immunity for violation of First Amendment rights, thus disproving Defendants' claim. (How dumb can Cardozo and McCann get?)

Reason 2

a. It is distressing that the District Court judge overturned the jury's decision.
b. If the trial judge can overrule a jury, what is the point of having a jury trial?
c. The jury has the duty to judge the law as well as the facts (see Exhibit D of Heicklen, Memorandum of Law, October 10, 2009, in the Reproduced Record).

d. This decision of the District Court judge to overrule the jury's decision shows the Courts' contempt of the jury system.
e. It also illustrates that the courts are in collusion with the police to protect them in their criminal activities. If this becomes common it is the end of constitutional government
f. That District Court judge should be removed from the judiciary.

Reason 3

a. The Court of Appeals Opinion discussed some critical issues.
b. The District Court Judge stated:
    i. "If this occurred and the jury finds that it occurred the way the plaintiff says it occurred, there is no immunity."
    ii. "It is the law, because the factual dispute here, the factual dispute has to be resolved before there can be a finding of whether or not there is qualified immunity."
c. The court explained, *inter alia*, that "probable cause exists when the facts and circumstances within the knowledge of the police officers at the time the arrest was made were sufficient to warrant a person of reasonable prudence to believe that a violation or a crime has been committed by the person arrested."
d. In his charge to the jury, the District Court Judge stated:

> "The arrest at issue must have been made...on probable cause. Also, resisting arrest does not accordance with the law. Namely, that it was based require that the person being arrested use force or

violence. It is enough if he engages in his conduct with the intent of preventing the officer from effecting the authorized arrest of himself. Accordingly, on the issue of the alleged Constitutional violation, making an unlawful arrest for disorderly conduct or resisting arrest, if you determine that there was no probable cause to arrest plaintiff on either of those charges [and that defendants' actions were a proximate cause of injury to Zellner], your verdict will be in favor of the plaintiff and against the defendants, as to the Federal Section 1983 false arrest cause of action. However, if you determine that . . . there was probable cause to arrest plaintiff for either disorderly conduct or resisting arrest, then the arrest would be lawful and your verdict must be in favor of the defendants with regard to the charge of false arrest."

e. The Court of Appeals further stated that:

> "Once the jury has resolved any disputed facts that are material to the qualified immunity issue, the ultimate determination of whether the officer's conduct was objectively reasonable is to be made by the court."

f. The Court further stated that:

> "Qualified immunity is an affirmative defense. See Gomez v. Toledo, 446 U.S. 635, 640 (1980). [B] ecause qualified immunity is an affirmative defense, it is incumbent upon the defendant to plead, and

adequately develop, a qualified immunity defense during pretrial proceedings so that the trial court can determine . . . which facts material to the qualified immunity defense must be presented to the jury to determine its applicability once the case has gone to trial. Blissett v. Coughlin, 66 F.3d 531, 538 (2d Cir. 1995) (emphasis added). To the extent that a particular finding of fact is essential to a determination by the court that the defendant is entitled to qualified immunity, it is the responsibility of the defendant to request that the jury be asked the pertinent question. See, *e.g., id.* If the defendant does not make such a request, he is not entitled to have the court, in lieu of the jury, make the needed factual finding. See, e.g., Kerman, 374 F.3d at 120; see also Warren, 906 F.2d at 76 ("the jury should decide these issues on special interrogatories") quoting Anderson v. Creighton, 483 U.S. at 641)." "'Arguable' probable cause must not be misunderstood to mean 'almost' probable cause." Jenkins v. City of New York, 478 F.3d 76, 87 (2d Cir. 2007). The essential inquiry in determining whether qualified immunity is available to an officer accused of false arrest is whether it was objectively reasonable for the officer to conclude that probable cause existed. See Anderson[v. Creighton], 483 U.S. at 644 . . . . There should be no doubt that probable cause remains the relevant standard. If officers of reasonable competence would have to agree that the information possessed by the officer at the time of arrest did not add up to probable cause, the fact that it came close does not immunize the officer. Jenkins

v. City of New York, 478 F.3d at 87 (emphasis added)"

In summary close to probable cause does not immunize the officer. The question is who is to decide probable cause? Some Court decisions say that the Court should decide and some say that other police officers should decide.

Plaintiff objects to both methods and prefers that the jury make the decision. To let other police officers make the decision is absurd. They would always support their fellow officers (This is known among police as the blue wall of silence.) Preferable to other police officers making the decision is to have the trial judge make the decision. However there is a difficulty here as shown in Zellner's case. The police and judges are in criminal collusion and cannot be trusted to make honest decisions. The best solution, in Plaintiff's view, is to have an impartial jury make the decision.

Zellner further states:

a. "Thus a court may grant a motion for judgment as a matter of law 'only if it can conclude that, with credibility assessments made against the moving party, a reasonable juror would have been compelled to accept the view of the moving party.'"
b. "The Standard for Judgment as a Matter of Law in considering a motion for judgment as a matter of law, the district court must draw all reasonable inferences in favor of the nonmoving party, and it may not make credibility determinations or weigh the evidence. . ." "Credibility determinations, the weighing of the evidence, and the drawing of legitimate inferences from the facts are jury functions, not those of a judge." . . . "Thus, although the court should review the record as a whole, it must disregard all evidence favorable to the

moving party that the jury is not required to believe. Reeves v. Sanderson Plumbing, 530 U.S. 133, 150-51 (2000) (quoting Anderson v. Liberty Lobby, Inc., 477 U.S. 242, 255 (1986)) (emphases ours). Thus, a court may grant a motion for judgment as a matter of law "only if it can conclude that, with credibility assessments made against the moving party and all inferences drawn against the moving party, a reasonable juror would have been compelled to accept the view of the moving party." Piesco v. Koch, 12 F.3d 332, 343 (2d Cir. 1993) (emphasis added). In ruling on a such motion, the court must bear in mind that the jury is free to believe part and disbelieve part of any witness's testimony. See, e.g., Fiacco v. City of Rensselaer, 783 F.2d 319, 325 (2d Cir. 1986), cert. denied, 480 U.S. 922 (1987); see also Haywood v. Koehler, 78 F.3d 101, 105 (2d Cir. 1996) (jurors are "free to accept bits of testimony from several witnesses and to make reasonable inferences from whatever testimony they credit[]"). Incontrovertible evidence relied on by the moving party, such as a relevant videotape whose accuracy is unchallenged, should be credited by the court on such a motion if it so utterly discredits the opposing party's version that no reasonable juror could fail to believe the version advanced by the moving party. See Scott v. Harris, 127 S. Ct. 1769, 1775-76 (2007) (so holding with respect to proceedings on summary judgment); see generally Reeves, 530 U.S. at 150 ("the standard for granting summary judgment 'mirrors' the standard for judgment as a matter of law, such that 'the inquiry under each is the same'" (quoting Anderson v. Liberty Lobby, Inc., 477 U.S. at 250-51)). The court is not permitted to find as a fact a proposition that is contrary to a finding made by the jury. See, e.g., Smith v. Lightning Bolt Productions, Inc., 861 F.2d 363, 367 (2d Cir. 1988) (court "cannot . . . substitute its judgment for that of the jury" (internal quotation marks omitted)); see also Leblanc-Sternberg v. Fletcher, 67 F.3d 412, 430 (2d Cir. 1995) ("In ruling on the motion by [one codefendant] for judgment as a matter of law, . . . the court was required to view the evidence in the light most favorable to the [individual] plaintiffs"; "whatever its own view of the facts may have been, the court was not entitled to substitute its view for adequately supported findings that were implicit in the jury's verdict" against another defendant cert. denied, 518 U.S. 1017 (1996). Nor is the court permitted to make findings on factual questions not submitted to the jury where those findings take the evidence in the light most favorable to the moving party, rather than the opposing party. See, e.g., Kerman, 374 F.3d at 120."

In the present case, defendants seek to defend the district court's decision granting them qualified immunity as a matter of law by asserting that they had actual or arguable probable cause to arrest Zellner (a) for disorderly conduct in violation of N.Y. Penal Law § 240.20(5), as charged, and (b) for other violations not charged, to wit, disorderly conduct in violation of subsections (6) and (7) of § 240.20 and obstructing the troopers' functioning in violation of Penal Law § 195.05. We conclude, applying the above principles, that the record does not support qualified immunity on any of these bases."

I. ***RESPONDEAT SUPERIOR***

Respondiat Superior is a centuries old common law legal doctrine that an employer is responsible for employee actions undertaken during the course of their employment. In 3 cases in 2004 this court added the requirement of personal involvement [Blyden v. Mancusi, 186 F.3d 252 (2d Cir. 2004); Patterson v. County of Oneida, 375 F.3d 206 (2d Cir. 2004); Feingold v. New York, 366 F.3d 138 (2d Cir. 2004)].

Judge Wood of the U. S. District Court of the Southern District of New York, states that two reasons to hold *respondent superior* responsible are: "creating a policy or custom under which constitutional practices occurred" or "the defendant was grossly negligent in supervising subordinates who committed the wrongful acts." (**ORDER** of Judge Kimba Wood, Original Complaint, U. S. District Court, S. D. N. Y., Docket # CV 02457, March 11, 2008).

Judge Koeltl states that "Personal involvement of defendants in alleged constitutional deprivations is a prerequisite to an award of damages under §1983." Back v. Hastings on Hudson Union Free Sch, Dist, 365 F.3d 107, 122 (2nd Cir. 2004) (quoting McKinnon v. Patterson, 568 F.2d 930, 934 (2nd Cir. 1977); See also Ashcroft v. Iqbal, 129 S. Ct. 1937, 1952 (2009)."

Appellant claims that Commissioner Kelly, the *respondiat superior*, either was aware of procedures in his jurisdictions and approved or permitted them; or, if not aware, he was negligent in performing his supervisory duties. It is inconceivable that the *respondiat superior* was not aware of the flagrant violations of his employees. In any event, the facts of the matter are for a jury, not a judge, to decide. That is what juries do.

Appellant expects to prove either complicity or negligence of *respondiat superior* if he gets the opportunity to question witnesses in front of a jury.

Additional opinions are given in Reproduced Record J. Heicklen **RESPONSE MEMORANDUM OF LAW TO REPLY MEMORANDUM OF LAW IN FURTHER SUPPORT OF DEFENDANTS' MOTION TO DISMISS OR, IN THE ALTERNATIVE, FOR SUMMARY JUDGMENT**, 10-19-2009.

It is not required of the moved party (Plaintiff) to support his allegations or lack thereof. It is required that the movant prove beyond any doubt that Defendant Kelly was not involved [Conley v. Gibson, 355 U.S. 41 (1957)]. Almost no doubt does not qualify [Anderson v. Creighton, 483 U.S. 635 at 644 (1987); Jenkins v. City of New York, 478 F.3d at 87, 2d Cir. (2007)]. Plaintiff's claim that Defendant Kelly was involved are based on both the specific actions of the police at the incident and because of repeated general behavior of the police.

Specific actions of the police

The demonstration was publicized widely well in advance. It was covered by all types of media and received worldwide coverage. It was organized by Rabbi Avi Weiss, one of the most highly respected rabbis in the U. S. It is clear that the arrests were well orchestrated in advance. Present were many police officers, including those from the Patrol Boro Manhattan South Task Force and legal advisors.

The rabbis congregated on the stairs and gave speeches without police interference. The rabbis sat on the stairs and were ordered to move several times before being placed under arrest. After the arrests, a John Doe Officer announced on a bullhorn that the demonstration was over. It is not the prerogative of the police to end a peaceful demonstration. Plaintiff alleges that this would not have been done without Commissioner Kelly's permission.

In order to end the demonstration the police had moved all the standing demonstrators 35 feet back, so that they could not be seen from the street. None of the standing demonstrators, except Plaintiff, were arrested. Plaintiff originally had moved back 35 feet with the other standing demonstrators, but when he realized that he could not be seen from the street, he moved forward 22 feet, but still 13 feet behind the sitting demonstrators. Plaintiff was ordered to move back with the other standing demonstrators or be arrested.

After some discussion with the police, he was placed "under arrest."

J. FEDERAL LAW AND RIGHTS

Several of Petitioner's federal rights were violated. These are:

a. The right to peaceably assemble guaranteed by Amendment I of the U. S. Constitution.
b. "In suits at common law...the right of trial by jury shall be preserved" as guaranteed by Amendment VII of the U. S. Constitution.
c. Amendment XIV, Sec 1 of the U. S. Constitution states: "nor shall any State deprive any person of life, liberty, or property without due process of law."
d. Petitioner was kidnapped by the police (a federal offense: 18 U.S.C. §1201), but was not able to recover damages or receive justice in the New York State courts.

K. BAD FAITH

The defendants lied about the facts. They submitted a tampered video, which conflicts with the police deposition. Judge Koeltl lied about the facts. He did not know what they were. The purpose of a court is to let the jury determine the facts. Plaintiff has been denied this constitutional right.

Judge Koeltl never pretended to provide a fair trial. He never required defendants to provide discovery. He accepted the Defendants' statements as factually true, even though they lied continually about them.

Judge Koeltl claims that the tampered video shows irrefutable proof of the innocence of the police. Actually the tampered tape shows irrefutable proof that Plaintiff was never placed under arrest (this part of the incident was deleted from the tape), but was kidnapped by the police.

Plaintiff was denied a jury trial as required by the U. S. Constitution.

L. IMPORTANCE OF THIS CASE

This case is not just about an isolated incident of police and judicial malpractice. It is representative of the widespread and ongoing abuse of citizens by the New York City Police and the New York City and State courts.

Incidents that Appellant witnessed in these courts involving people who had neither the mental nor financial means to protect themselves were disturbing. These abuses must be stopped.

Furthermore this case is about hate, particularly the hatred of Jews, which is now widespread in the United States and around the world. The police were trying to terminate a peaceful demonstration against the President of Iran.

The President of Iran is the modern day reincarnation of Adolph Hitler. He believes the Muslims are the master race, that the state of Israel should be obliterated, and the Jews removed therefrom. He addressed the UN General Assembly several times, where he advocated the destruction of Israel.

M. MOTIONS (RELIEF SOUGHT)

Appellant moves that the Circuit Court reverse the decision of the District Court and order the District Court to proceed promptly with trial.

Appellant moves Judge Koeltl be recused from trying this case and a new judge be appointed.

XXXI. APPEALS COURT RESPONSE

I received no response from the Court of Appeals: Second Circuit. Therefore, on August 2, 2010, I wrote the following to Deputy clerk Ahronda Crossman:

"On July 2, 2010, I sent 10 copies of **APPELLANT'S BRIEF IN SUPPORT OF APPEAL** to the Circuit Court via United Parcel Service. I have not had an acknowledgment from your office that you received these documents."

"Please acknowledge receipt of these documents and send a schedule for Appellee's response, my reply, and possible oral argument dates. Also let me know if you need any further documents from me at this time."

"Thank you for your cooperation."

I received no reply. Therefore on September 7, 2010, I wrote to Catherine O'Hagan Wolfe, Clerk of Court, with a copy to Dennis Jacobs, Chief Judge:

"On July 2, 2010, I sent 10 copies of **APPELLANT'S BRIEF IN SUPPORT OF APPEAL** to the Circuit Court via United Parcel Service. I have not had an acknowledgment form your office that you received these documents."

"Please acknowledge receipt of these documents and send a schedule for Appellee's response, my reply, and possible oral argument dates. Also let me know if you need any further documents from me at this time."

"Thank you for your cooperation."

I received a reply to this letter with some misinformation. So I wrote again to Ms. Crossman on September 16, 2010:

"I have received your letters of your Amended Caption Notice and Case Status Update. There appears to be a mixup in cases. Originally I submitted a complaint to the district court with all of the named defendants you listed. All of the named defendants, except the police officers, were removed because of immunity to prosecution. I filed an amended complaint with the only defendants being Raymond Kelly, Jason Toala, and 3 John Does. It is case Docket # 08–Civ.–2457 (JGK) from the amended complaint that is being appealed."

"In your previous correspondence and on the Court of Appeals **ORDER**, the Court of Appeals Docket # 10–1251 is given. I have continued to use this number. The Short Title for the case should be: Julian Heicklen v. New York City Police. Also Julian is spelled with one letter n."

"The cover page for my appeal brief is correct as submitted, so I have made no changes. However, I am concerned that the district court may have sent you an incorrect reproduced record. Please send me a list of documents submitted by the district court, so I can check for accuracy."

"You list Scott Nathan Shorr, Assistant Corporation Counsel, as the Appellees' attorney. This is news to me. The district court case defense counsel was Max McCann. I have received no correspondence from the appellees' attorneys since I filed my brief. Please inform me who they are, and if they have made an appearance."

"I have not sent a copy of this letter to the Office of the New York City Corporation Counsel, since I do not know to whom it should be sent."

XXXII. REPLY TO APPELLEES' RESPONSE

Appellees submitted a **RESPONSE** to my **BRIEF IN SUPPORT OF APPEAL**. It and my **REPLY** were as follows:

A. TECHNICAL ERRORS IN APPELLEES' RESPONSE

Appellant has received a **RESPONSE** dated November 9, 2010, from Scott Shorr, Senior Counsel, Appeals Division, The City of New York, Law Department, 100 Church Street, New York, NY 10007, to his **BRIEF IN SUPPORT OF APPEAL**. There are numerous technical errors in Mr. Shorr's response. These are:

a. There is no Table of Contents as required by FRAP 28(a)(2)
b. There is no table of authorities as required by FRAP 28(a)(3)
c. There was no cover page as required by FRAP 32 (a)(2)
d. The first page is not red as required by FRAP 32 (a)(2)
e. Caption of the case is not given as required by FRAP 32(a)(2)
f. The text is not double spaced as required by FRAP 32(a)(4)
g. The text statements are not numbered as required by FRAP ?? (could not locate the rule)
h. An appearance is given for Julie Steiner, but none for Scott Shorr as required by FRAP ?? (could not locate the rule)
i. No certificate of service is provided as required by FRAP 25(d)

FRAP Rule 31(a)(1) requires a response time within 30 days of submission of Appellant's brief. Appellant's brief was mailed on July 2, 2010. Mr. Shorr's **RESPONSE** is dated November 9, 2010, which is well over the 30 day limit. Appellant's **REPLY** is dated December 16, 2010, which technically exceeds the 14 day reply time. However Appellant was in California from November 5–15, 2010, and in Florida from November 25–December 11, 2010, so that he has responded in the 14 days available to him to prepare a **REPLY**.

Furthermore, since Mr. Shorr has not made an appearance nor filed a **RESPONSE** on time, his **RESPONSE** is not admissible. Appellant Heicklen is not required to reply at all.

B. CRIMINAL CASE DISMISSED

All of the allegations in the police deposition were lies, as the video tape shows. The criminal case against Appellant Heicklen has been dismissed by the Criminal Court of New York in the interest of justice. The District Attorney of New York realized that there was no legitimate reason for Appellant Heicklen's arrest on April 17, 2007.

C. TAINTED EVIDENCE

The video submitted as evidence was tampered as proven by two facts:

a. Part of the sound track is muffled or missing.
b. The time of arrest given in the police deposition would place Appellant Heicklen as the first person arrested. The video shows that he was the last person arrested. The part of the video where

Heicklen twice personally was placed "under arrest" has been deleted.

D. LIES BY MR. SHORR

The first lie by Mr. Shorr appears in the third paragraph on page 2 of his letter where he states: "Among the protesters were approximately 25 rabbis, who sat on one step and the landing closest to the First Avenue sidewalk, blocking pedestrian traffic." The rabbis were sitting on several steps and not on the landing, except where the landing was the top step.

The second lie appears in paragraph 5 where he states: "Plaintiff stood on the stairway,.." Heicklen is not on the stairway. He is on the landing behind the rabbis. Heicklen never stood on the stairway, and the video never shows him standing on the stairway.

The third lie appears in the last paragraph on page 2. Mr Shorr states: "Pedestrians attempted to walk through the crowd of protesters assembled on the stairway and landings." The word attempted implies that the pedestrians were obstructed. That is not the case. Pedestrians walked through the standing demonstrators unobstructed.

In the last paragraph on page 2, Mr Shorr agrees that Lieutenant Wolf is only arresting the demonstrators on the sidewalk staircase, not the standing demonstrators behind them. Except for Heicklen, no standing demonstrator was arrested.

On the first paragraph on top of page 3, Mr. Shorr states: "Among the protestors, plaintiff remained on the stairway,..." Another lie. Heicklen was never on the stairway occupied by the rabbis at any time. For one thing there was no room left for any standing demonstrators.

In the second paragraph on page 3, Mr. Shorr states correctly (strange as that may seem) that Lieutenant Wolf warned "'the ones in the back' that if you do not want to be arrested, you're going to have to clear the stairs now." It applies only to the protesters (rabbis) who are sitting on the stairs. Heicklen was 13 feet behind the stairs and was not included.

Mr. Shorr lied again in the first paragraph under **2. Plaintiff's Arrest**, where he states: "...35 feet behind the landing where the rabbis had been seated." The rabbis were not seated on a landing, but on the first set of stairs, which was separated from the second set of stairs by the landing.

Mr. Shorr states at the end of the first paragraph under Item 2 on page 3 that: "...if he did not leave the landing, he would be arrested." Almost another correct statement. Mr. Shorr is on a roll. By Mr. Shorr's own admission, this is the point where Heicklen is placed under arrest. If Heicklen had moved, he would not have been arrested.

In the next paragraph, Mr. Shorr states correctly that "...if he did not leave the landing, he would be arrested." Apparently Heicklen was not arrested at this point. This was the second notice that Heicklen could move back and avoid arrest.
By Mr. Shorr's own testimony, which agrees with the video at this point, Heicklen was not placed under arrest until receiving two personal warnings after all the sitting demonstrators were arrested. I confirm that this is true.

In the first paragraph on page 4, Mr. Shorr quotes a law against congregating and refusal to disperse when ordered by police. I was not congregating. I was standing all alone. I was ordered to congregate, and refused to do so.

There were three reasons why I refused to congregate:

a. I have the Constitutional right to stand on a public passageway and demonstrate, as long as I do not interfere with anyone else. As the Court must be well aware, I have refused to move on 12 occasions at the U. S. District Court S. D. N.

Y. when ordered to do so by police officers. I refuse to cede my First Amendment rights. I have been arrested on several occasions there. The U. S. Attorney has dismissed all of those criminal cases in the interest of justice, just as the Criminal Court of Manhattan dismissed the criminal case arising out of the instant arrest.

b. Ordering me to move into a crowd of people demonstrating with signs, ram's horns, and other instruments is reckless endangerment. It is a crime committed by the police. If this Court really is interested in justice it will rule in my favor and have the arresting police officers removed from the police force for life.

c. The crowd of people in which I was ordered to join were committing the crime of blocking pedestrian traffic. I do not participate in criminal activity.

In paragraph 4 on page 4, Mr. Shorr argues for dismissal based on immunity and *respondeat superior.* I have discussed these at great length in my previous communications with this court.

In the second paragraph on page 5, Mr. Shorr resumes his lying. Heicklen was not congregating when placed under arrest. I was not blocking pedestrian traffic. I refused no order to disperse. I was not ordered to disperse. I was ordered to congregate.

Mr. Shorr defends Judge Koeltl's decisions at the end of page 5. These were decisions of fact, not of law. It may even be possible that they are correct. However I have demanded a jury trial. It is not the judge's duty to determine the facts. That is the prerogative of the jury. It is also the duty of the jury to judge the law (see Ch. 5), though that is not in contention here.

E. MISCONDUCT OF THE DEFENSE

The behavior of Judge Koeltl, the defense counsels, and the police have been abominable. They do not follow the court rules uniformly. They tamper with evidence. They lie under oath. They misrepresent the laws, court decisions, and the facts. Have they no shame? They certainly have not enhanced the reputation of the legal profession.

Our judicial system is completely corrupted. If we cannot rely on the rule of law, the only solution left will be armed rebellion. I dread such a solution and will not participate in it, but it seems inevitable.

This document is being released to the public, so that it can be fully aware of what occurs in our courts of injustice.

F. MOTION

Appellant moves that the U. S. Court of Appeals: Second Circuit reverse the decision of the District Court and award real and punitive damages to the Appellant, or at least return the case to the District Court for a jury trial under a different judge and defense counsel who tells the truth, if there is such a person.

G. PUBLIC DISCLOSURE

This document is being released to the public, so that it will know what transpires in the federal court system. At the time of the completion of this book (December 2010), there has been no decision from the Appeals Court. It will be several months for this to occur.

XXXIII. EPILOGUE

A. PENNSYLVANIA JUSTICE

The author of this book smoked marijuana cigarettes every Thursday at noon for 3 years from 1998–2000 in front of the main gate of the Pennsylvania State University in University Park, PA, or occasionally in front of the Centre County Courthouse, and announced what he was doing on a bullhorn. I do not advocate smoking marijuana and am not a user. However, I believe that is immoral to arrest someone for owning a vegetable, especially if I am going to have to pay for his room and board.

1. Arrest and pretrial hearing

I was arrested 6 times for these offenses; 4 times at Penn State and twice at the courthouse. My four arrests at Penn State University (Case numbers 1998–843, 1998–844, 1998–845, and 1998–556) were consolidated into one criminal trial for which I demanded a jury trial. The two criminal cases in front of the Courthouse were dismissed in the interests of Justice.

The pretrial conference was run by President Charles C. Brown, Jr., who was going to preside at jury selection and the trial. (Honest his name is Charlie Brown).

I pointed out that there was no laboratory report, only a statement from the state test lab that the substance tested was marijuana. I requested the reports, as well as the cigarettes so that we could have them tested independently. The prosecuting attorney, Stephen Sloane, replied that there were no reports other than the statement that the test was positive. He also did not have possession of the cigarette butts. I objected that this was not a report, only an opinion. Neither a report nor the evidence was ever submitted to the Court or the jury.

Counsels for both the prosecution and defense asked if they would be allowed to question prospective jurors before selection. Judge Charles C. Brown Jr. announced that he would ask the *voir dire* (questions to the jury) selected from questions that the two sides submitted. When asked if he would ask all of the questions, he said: "No, I'll pick and choose"

I pointed out that I intended to use jury nullification as a defense, *i. e.* I intended to ask the jury to find me not guilty and nullify the law. I showed U. S. Supreme Court decisions which upheld jury nullification as a defense. However Judge Brown said that he would not allow it, and would instruct the jury "...at the end of the trial that they have to follow the law." He also said that: "...this jury will be told that they must apply the law as I give it to them. They don't have any alternative but to apply the law."

2. Jury nullification

Of course Judge Brown was wrong. He was not ignorant of the law. He disdained it. In his mind, he was the law.

There is a long history of jury nullification. A prime purpose of the jury is to prevent enforcement of tyrannical laws. The purpose of the jury is not to enforce the law, but to see that Justice is done. Supposedly this is also the purpose of the courts, but juries were introduced because experience showed that judges did not deliver justice. A detailed discussion of jury nullification appears in Ch. V, pp. 42–45.

Nullification applies just as much in the states, including Pennsylvania. Article I of the Constitution of the Commonwealth of Pennsylvania states in Section 6: "Trial by jury shall be as heretofore, and the right thereof remain inviolate." Section 25 states: "To guard against transgressions of the high powers which we have delegated, we declare that everything in this article is excepted out of the general powers of government and shall forever remain inviolate." Taken together, these two sections mean that juries shall have the powers that they had "Heretofore." *i. e.* when the Constitution was adopted.

Judges usually do not inform the jury of this right. Even worse, some judges instruct the jury that it does not have the right to interpret or nullify the law, but only to determine the facts. Near the end of alcohol prohibition, juries refused to convict for alcohol violations. Has the time arrived for juries to do the same for marijuana violations?

3. Jury selection

For my my trial, the President Judge of the Court of Common Pleas of Centre County, PA, Charles C. Brown, Jr. decided to hear the case. He set the trial date for the first day of the Jewish New Year (Rosh Hashanah). Being Jewish, I informed him that I could not make that date. He said too bad, that is the date and it would not be changed.

Jury selection occurred on August 3, 1998. Judge Brown announced the trial date to be September 21, 1998, which was the first day of Rosh Hashanah, to the jury pool before jury selection. At jury selection, I objected to the date set for "trial of September 21, 2008, which is Rosh Hashanah which is the Jewish New Year. It interferes with my state and constitutional rights to freedom of religion and it also interferes with my state and constitutional rights to an impartial jury of my peers, because all the Jewish jurors are going to ask to be excused." Judge Brown responded: Well, that's something that I would have hoped would have been covered by Ms. Spotts beforehand." I responded that: " Well, I informed her. She had been informed." Ms. Spotts replied that she had no other dates available. Needless to say, all the Jews in the jury pool excused themselves.

I requested the opportunity to address the jury pool of 26 before jury selection, but both prosecuting and defense counsels were denied that opportunity, even though it had been allowed in the jury selection preceding mine.

After the jury was selected, Judge Brown changed the trial date to October 7, 1998, to be more convenient for me. This is how the Jews were kept off the jury.

PA law for compiling the jury master list is:

> (a) 42 Pa. C.S. §4521(a) Preparation of master list of prospective jurors.--
> (1) At least annually the jury selection commission shall prepare a master list of prospective jurors[.] that shall contain the most recent available address for prospective jurors.
> (2) The list shall also contain all voter registration lists for the county, which lists may be incorporated by reference, or names from such other lists which in the opinion of the commission will provide a number of names of prospective jurors which is equal to or greater than the number of names contained in the voter registration list.

In Centre County during the time of my trial (October 7, 1998), the jury master list used was the Occupation Assessment Tax (OAT) List for Centre County. This list contained 72,277 names compared to the voter registration list which contained 88,292 names on July 27, 2001. Thus the jury master list used was in violation of PA state law.

The reason the County Court used the Occupation Tax List was that it excluded almost all Penn State students and the unemployed, thus denying them a jury of their peers. According to the 2000 U. S. Census, the adult population of Centre County was 111,292, while the Penn State student population in Centre County was 37,860, excluding foreign students, during the academic year 2000–2001. Thus 35.1% of the adult U. S. population of Centre County was omitted from the jury master list. Not surprisingly, the

Centre County prison was overloaded with Penn State students and the unemployed.

In this way the two groups of people who might have more understanding of my case were prevented from serving on the jury. I faced a packed jury. Incidentally, the jurors were paid $9.00/day plus expenses. The federal minimum wage at that time (1998) was $5.15/hour ($41.20/day). The courts violate the law at will. After all, they are exempt from prosecution of their crimes.

4. The Trial

The jurors were forbidden to take notes during the trial. They were required to remember everything that was said during the day-long trial. They were not permitted to ask any questions nor allowed to write any questions for the judge to ask. Judge Brown also stated that he could not give the jury instructions in writing.

At the trial, the prosecution presented no evidence. Robert Wagner from the state crime lab testified that he tested my cigarettes for marijuana, and they tested positive. I asked him how he tested and was told by chromatography. I asked to see the chromatographs. He had none. I asked for retention times and did they compare with authentic samples of marijuana. He could not answer those questions. I asked him if the laboratory kept log books of the tests. He said yes. I asked to see them. He did not bring them, because it was against laboratory policy to show them. Marijuana is made of many compounds. I asked for which did he test. He said that he only tested for tetrahydrocannabinol, the psychedelic ingredient of marijuana.

According to PA statute 35 P. S. §780–102(b):

"Marijuana consists of all forms, species, and/or varieties of the genus *Cannabis sativa* whether growing or not;...but shall not include tetrahydrocannabinols..."

According to this law, tetrahydrocanabinol is excluded as a test for marijuana, because it is a licensed prescription drug sold under the trade name of Marinol. Thus even the claim that an illicit drug was found was false. I asked Judge Brown to read the law to the jury, but he refused to do so. The jury found me guilty without any evidence presented in court or even a knowledge of the state law. On appeal to the Middle District Superior Court of PA, the verdict was upheld.

In Judge Brown's charge to the jury he stated:

> "...I must tell you that the law that you will apply to this case is the law that I give to you, you must follow it. Even if you think I may have given you the wrong instructions or given you the law incorrectly, you still must follow the law as I give it to you."

Of course that is wrong. It is the duty of the jury to judge the law as well as the facts.

I was found guilty and sentenced to 120 days probation, required to attend drug rehabilitation, and fined $2000.00 plus court costs and supervision fees. However Judge Brown never signed the court order. Sentence was stayed until after the appeal process ran its course.

5. Appeals

I hired attorney Joseph Devecka to be my counsel for appeals. In his appeal to the Middle District Superior Court, he pointed out that:

> "At trial, the Commonwealth forensic scientist, Robert Wagner, gave testimony, R. R. p. 145a (R.R. = reproduced record). This forensic scientist had no advanced degrees, R.R. p. 149a, nor had he written any papers on testing marijuana, RR. p. 149a. The forensic scientist admitted that

all tests done to prove marijuana test for tetrahydrocanabinol, R.R. p. 158a. This forensic scientist also admitted that any other compounds in a sample are not tested for, R.R. p. 159a"

"No 1925(a) order was ever filed or served on appellate counsel and therefore there is no trial opinion."

"After the charge to the jury, Julian, acting as his own counsel at trial, raised an objection to the lower court's charge requesting that the trial court include the definition of marijuana in the charge R.R. p. 254a. The reason the charge was requested was that THC, tetrahydrocannabinol, was used at trial with the Commonwealth's witness, and the legal definition of marijuana specifically excludes THC, R.R. p. 255 and 35 P.S. §780–102(b) definition of marijuana."

The Middle District Superior Court of PA upheld the conviction. Petition for Allowance to Appeal was denied by the Middle District Supreme Court of PA.

6. Disposition of sentence

The Court never contacted me nor sent a signed order from Judge Brown, so I never reported for probation nor paid any fines or fees. More than four years after the trial, I was sued by the District Attorney for criminal contempt of court.

Judge Brown tried to enforce the sentence by charging me with criminal contempt of court for failing to serve my probation or pay my fines. However the court order was unsigned, and the time limit set by the Statute of Limitations (2 years) had passed.

Judge Brown claimed that the Statute of Limitations did not apply to contempt of court. I disagreed and filed an interlocutory appeal to the Superior Court. At the hearing of February 11, 2004, I pointed out that:

a. The criminal contempt charge was filed on November 22, 2002. This was the first contact with the Appellant from the District Attorney, the Court, or the Department of Probation and Parole since October 7, 1998. The Appellee's filing did not include a schedule of payments.
b. The lapse of time between contacts was 4 years and 46 days.
c. Appellant filed a **MOTION FOR DISMISSAL** on the grounds that there was no approved payment schedule. Appellee did not respond in writing, but claimed at the hearing that such contracts signed by the judge did exist. Judge Brown accepted this claim (**REPRODUCED RECORD**, pp. 100–103). Copies of the contracts were not given to Appellant nor introduced as evidence.
d. If this claim is correct, then default occurred on November 5, 1998. There was a lapse of 4 years and 17 days until filing by Appellee.
e. Statute of limitations for payments is one year (P.S. 42 Pa. C.S.A. §5523 One year Limitation).
f. Statute of limitations for prosecution of misdemeanors, summary offenses, and some felonies is two years. P. S. 42 Pa. C.S.A. §5552(a) General Rule states: "Except as otherwise provided in this subsection, a prosecution for an offense other than murder or voluntary manslaughter must be commenced within two years after it is committed."
g. Pa. R.C.P. 706, Fines or Costs does not mention the statutes of limitations. Specifically, it does not exempt fines or costs from the statutes of limitations.
h. In his **OPINION** of May 16, 2003 (Exhibit A of **BRIEF OF APPELLANT**), Judge Brown claimed that Appellant did not commit a crime or offense. Then why has Appellant been accused of criminal contempt, which is a

crime? The U. S. Supreme Court stated in Headnote [4] of Bloom v. Illinois 391 U. S. 194; 88 S. Ct. 1477; 20 L. Ed. 2d 522: 1968 U. S. Lexus 2993 that : "Criminal contempt is a crime in the ordinary sense, a violation of the law, a public wrong punishable by fine or imprisonment or both, irrespective of whether the contemptuous conduct may violate other provisions of the criminal law; the role of criminal contempt and that of many ordinary criminal laws seem identical--protection of the institutions of the government and enforcement of their mandates."236

i. Appellant pointed out that in the Marks Appeal 144, Pa. Super. 556; 20 A.2d 242; (1941), Mark's conviction was overturned by the PA Superior Court, because the statute of limitations time limit had been exceeded (**BRIEF OF APPELLANT** pp. 4–5).

The Middle District Superior Court remanded the case back to Centre County Court, because an interlocutory appeal was not appropriate It was clear from my appeal that the statute of limitations did apply, so Judge Brown dropped the matter. I never served my sentence nor paid any fines or court costs. I never heard from Judge Brown again.

7. Suit Against Jury Commission

After my trial was over, I filed a lawsuit against the Centre County Jury Commission in Commonwealth Court The Commonwealth Court claimed that it did not have jurisdiction and sent the case to the Centre County Court of Common Pleas. Charles Brown, the President Judge of the Centre County Court of Common Pleas was also Chair of the Jury Commission. Not surprisingly, this case is still (December 2010) sitting on the judge's desk waiting for a trial date.

On August 23, 2001, I filed a petition with the Commonwealth Court of PA (Case No. 44 M. D. 2001) to enforce the law for jury master list selection in Centre County, PA under 16 Pa.C.S.A. §460(a), 42 Pa.C.S.A. §4521, 42 Pa.C.S.A. §4522, 42 Pa.C.S.A. §4523, 42 Pa.C.S.A. §4524, 65 P.S. §66.2, 65 P.S. §121, Article I, Section 9 of the Pennsylvania Constitution, Amendment VI to the U. S. Constitution, and Amendment XIV, Section 1 to the U. S. Constitution. The Defendants were the three jury commissioners: Judge Charles C. Brown, Jr., Ruth DeWitt, and Ann Lose, as well as Maxine Ishler and Barbara Gallo, who were officials of the Centre County court of Common Pleas. For detailed information see http://www.personal.psu.edu/faculty/j/p/jph13/PleadingJuryComm.html

The primary statute that was being violated by the Centre County Court of Common Pleas was:

> 42 Pa. C.S. § 4521(a) Preparation of master list of prospective jurors.--
> (1) At least annually the jury selection commission shall prepare a master list of prospective jurors[.] that shall contain the most recent available address for prospective jurors.
> (2) The list shall also contain all voter registration lists for the county, which lists may be incorporated by reference, or names from such other lists which in the opinion of the commission will provide a number of names of prospective jurors which is equal to or greater than the number of names contained in the voter registration list.

B. JUSTICE IN OTHER STATES

New York state and the Commonwealth of Pennsylvania are not the only states in which the courts have failed. Probably every state, as well as the federal courts, has its horror stories. These often result from the desire of judges and prosecuting attorneys to get convictions rather than deliver justice. Prosecutors are known for persuading criminal witnesses to lie under oath in order to get reduced sentences for themselves. Bargaining for reduced sentences by incriminating others is a dangerous practice. Furthermore, defendants often do not receive an adequate defense.

While I have no first hand knowledge of court misconduct in states other than New York and Pennsylvania, there is plenty of evidence for it. The Innocence Project (http://www.innocenceproject.org/) has freed many innocent prisoners. These include:

Larry Johnson, misidentified and sentenced to life in prison in Missouri..

David Shepard served nine years in a NJ prison for a crime he did not commit.

Clarence Harrison freed by DNA evidence after serving nearly 18 years in a Georgia prison.

Bernard Webster served 20 years in a Maryland prison based on forensic misconduct.

Ronald Taylor served 12 years in a Texas prison for faulty lab tests before trial.

Orlando Boquette misidentified and wrongfully convicted in Florida in1982.

Bruce Godschalk served over 14 years in prison after giving a coerced confession.

John Restivo wrongfully convicted in NY based on forensic misconduct.

Dean Cage misidentified and wrongfully convicted in Illinois.

Frederick Daye served 10 years in a California prison for a crime he did not commit.

Rickey Johnson served 25 years in a Louisiana prison for a crime he did not commit.

William Gregory was the first person to be exonerated by DNA evidence in Kentucky.

Others who have been exonerated are:

Pete Williams was misidentified by a rape victim and served 21 years in prison.

Calvin Johnson, served 16 years in prison. Now (2009) he serves as Chairman of the Board of the Georgia Innocence Project.

John White was convicted of a rape he did not do and was sentenced to life in prison. It was 29 years later before he was released based on DNA evidence. The real rapist was in the identifying lineup, was released, and committed another rape.

Robert Clark was convicted of a rape committed in 1993 and served 12 years in prison before he was exonerated by DNA evidence.

Steven Barnes of Oneida County, NY was exonerated in January, 2009, after spending nearly 20 years in prison for a crime he did not commit. In 1989, at age 23, he was wrongfully convicted of the 1985 rape and murder of a high school student (private correspondence from the Innocence Project, November 20, 2009.)

Ernest Sonnier of Harris County, TX, was released from prison on August 7, 2009 after serving 23 years of a life sentence for a rape that he did not commit (private correspondence from the Innocence Project, November 20, 2009).

Those not freed include:

Cameron Todd Willingham was convicted in 1992 of setting a fire that killed his three children. He spent 12 years in prison in Texas and was executed in 2004. A recent reinvestigation concluded in

2009 that he was innocent (David Grann, New Yorker magazine, September 7, 2009, pp.42–63).

William Osborne, a convicted rapist, requested post conviction DNA testing , paid at his own expense, to exonerate himself. The U. S. Supreme Court (District Attorney's Office for the Third Judicial District v. Osborne, June 18, 2009 (No. 08–6) 521 F. 3d 1118) denied Osborne this opportunity in a 5–4 decision based on the argument that there is no U. S. Constitutional provision for this. It is true that the U. S. Constitution does not guarantee the rights of life, liberty, and the pursuit of happiness. Those provisions are in the Declaration of Independence and were the reason for the revolutionary war by the British colonies. If those provisions do not apply, why do we need a judiciary at all?

In April, 2009, the Innocence Project reported that, based on new DNA evidence, Timothy Cole was exonerated posthumously in Texas for a rape that he did not commit, and that Miguel Roman was exonerated in Connecticut for a murder he did not commit after serving 21 years.

The Innocence Project (http://www.innocenceproject.org/) has saved inmates from execution for crimes that they did not commit. Among them are:

Frank Lee Smith, Earl Washington, and Ron Williamson [Reason magazine, Vol 47, No. 7, p. 10 (December, 2009)].

Bernard Baran served 22 years on dubious child molestation charges, but the prosecutor who convicted him was promoted to judge. Baran was raped in prison. His conviction was based on videos in which testimony by children denying being molested by Baran was removed. Also children who denied abuse were repeatedly questioned after denials until they gave affirmative action, for which they were rewarded with candy. The prosecutor, Caniel Ford, is now a judge on the Massachusetts Superior Court [Reason magazine, Vol 47, No. 7, p. 36–37 (December, 2009)].

Canton, IL cab driver Lloyd E. Miller was convicted of the murder of Janice May in 1955 and sentenced to death. Subsequently the U. S. Supreme Court unanimously reversed Miller's conviction because the prosecution had used false evidence with an almost incredible disregard for U. S. standards of fair trial. Said Justice Stewart: "More than 30 years ago, this court held that the 14th Amendment cannot tolerate a state criminal conviction obtained by the knowing use of false evidence. There has been no deviation from that principle. There can be no retreat." More details of this crime can be found at: http://www.time.com/time/magazine/article/0,9171,899431,00.html.

Troy A. Davis was convicted of murder in Georgia and sentenced to die on September 23, 2008. Mr. Davis claimed that he was not at the scene of the crime. The prosecution offered no murder weapon, DNA or fingerprints tying Mr. Davis to the killing. Since the trial, seven key witnesses have recanted their testimony saying that they were bullied by investigators to lie under oath. (New York Times, September 13, 2008, page A16). His appeal to the U. S. Supreme Court was heard on December 9, 2008. On June 1, 2009, in the New York Times, p. A21, Bob Barr, a former Comgressman, discussed this case and pointed out that there was no intent in legislation passed by Congress to prohibit the courts from reviewing cases of this sort. As of this writing (December 17, 2008), no decision has been announced.

On June 18, 2009, the U. S. Supreme Court ruled 5–4 that William G. Osborne, a prisoner in Alaska, could not receive post-conviction DNA testing at his own expense. Chief Justice Roberts, who sided with the majority, acknowledged that the "unparalled ability" of DNA testing "both to exonerate the wrongly convicted and to identify the guilty." The five Justices that voted against post-conviction DNA testing were Roberts, Alito, Thomas, Kennedy, and Scalia. They concluded that it is more important for a criminal case to reach finality than to determine guilt or innocence. Why these people are referred to as "Justices" is a mystery of the English language. For more details, see the New York Times, June 19, 2009, pp. A1, A18, and A26.

Dewey Bozella was released on October 28, 2009, in Poughkeepsie, NY, when his murder conviction was overturned. He had spent 26 years in prison as reported in the New York Times, October 29, 2009. He had been convicted with tainted testimony, withheld evidence, and a botched investigation.

Others exonerated are reported in the winter, 2009 issue, Volume 5, #2 of the Innocene Project. They are: George Rodriquez, Josiah Sutton, Kevin Byrd, Kenneth Ireland, Joseph Abbitt, James Lee Woodward, and Lawrence McKinney.

Fortunately there has been retreat. On April 6, 2000, Robert Tanner of the Associated Press reported "Across the nation, dozens of convicts go free after a new look at evidence proves them innocent. A police scandal unravels in Los Angeles, with 99 people framed and convicted. Illinois stops all executions after 13 condemned men are freed." For more information see http://findarticles.com/p/articles/mi_qn4182/is_20000406/ai_n10136241?tag=rel.r In January, 2003, outgoing Governor George Ryan of Illinois commuted the sentences of all death row inmates, because of the possibility of error in their trials. His decision affected 156 inmates on death row and 11 others sentenced to death, but who were not in custody. Ryan pardoned four death row inmates after determining they had been tortured into confessing crimes they did not commit. For more information see: http://www.cnn.com/2003/LAW/01/11/illinois.death.row/. Ironically, in 2006 Governor Ryan was convicted of sweeping federal corruption charges.

Since 1989, more than 250 innocent prisoners have been exonerated by DNA ("The Innocence Project in Print." Yeshiva University Law School, Vol 6. Issue 1 [Summer 2010]) — plus more than 200 other exonerations that did not involve DNA. For a fuller discussion see: http://www.latimes.com/news/opinion/la-oe-ross11jun11,0,3153812.story?coll=la- opinion-rightrail.

Samuel Gross and Barbara O'Brien know basic facts about all defendants who were sentenced to death from 1973 on in the United States, and they know which of them were exonerated. From these data they estimated that the frequency of wrongful death sentences in the United States is at least 2.3% (http://papers.ssrn.com/sol3/papers.cfm?abstract_id=996629). Samuel Gross also points out that if only 1% of criminal convictions are wrong, then 20,000 prisoners in the United States are innocent: (http://www.latimes.com/news/opinion/la-oe-gross11jun11,0,3153812.story?coll=la-opinion-rightrail).

At least three states have reintroduced debtors prison, even though the U. S. Supreme Court ruled it unconstitutional in 1970. In the April 6, 2009, edition of the New York Times, it reported three such cases on its editorial page. Edwina Nowlin, a poor Michigan resident could not reimburse a juvenile detention center $104 per month. She was sent to prison. The American Civil Liberties Union managed to get her released after 28 days in prison. According to the New York Times, until a few years ago, the police of Gulfport, MS, did sweeps of the city's predominantly

African-American neighborhoods, identified people with unpaid fines, and put them in jail until they "sat off" their fines. The city ended the practice after it was sued.

According to Stephen Bright, President of the Southern Center for Human Rights, in Georgia, people who cannot pay fines are often sent to jail for nonpayment. One woman was locked up for 8 months because she could not pay her $705 fine.

Aside from the illegality and inhumanity of debtors prison, it is a financially losing strategy for the governments. It cost about $50/day to keep a person in county jail. Michigan spent about $1400 because it could not collect $704. Georgia spent about $12,000 because it could not collect $705.

C. U. S. FEDERAL COURT JUSTICE

The classic case of the disregard by the U. S. Supreme Court for the U. S. Constitution is that of Bush v. Gore 531 U. S. 98 (2000). In 2000, Albert Gore sued Katherine Harris in the Florida Supreme Court [772 So.2d 1243 (2000)] as the representative of the State of Florida. In Bush v. Gore, George Bush petitioned the U. S. Supreme Court to intervene in that case.

Amendment XI to the U. S. Constitution states in full : "The Judicial power of the United States shall not be construed to extend to any suit in law or equity, commenced or prosecuted against one of the United States by Citizens of another State, or by Citizens or Subjects of any Foreign State."

Albert Gore, a citizen of the state of Tennessee was suing the state of Florida. According to Amendment XI, the U. S. courts could not intervene in that case. Yet the U. S. Supreme Court did so, in violation of Amendment XI of the U. S. Constitution. It illegally appointed George Bush the 43rd President of the United States.

A discussion of the case is given in: http://www.law.cornell.edu/background/election/. Even if the U. S. Supreme Court had jurisdiction, it was in error in its decision. In their dissent, Justice Stevens, with whom Justice Ginsburg and Justice Breyer joined, stated "The Constitution assigns to the States the primary responsibility for determining the manner of selecting the Presidential electors." Justice Stevens concluded his dissent with the statement: "Although we may never know with complete certainty the identity of the winner of this year's Presidential election, the identity of the loser is perfectly clear. It is the Nation's confidence in the judge as an impartial guardian of the rule of law."

For the presidential election of 2000, Congress determined that the day for Congress to receive electoral vote reports from the fifty States and the District of Columbia, and, if necessary, to entertain, adjudicate and resolve objections thereto, was January 6, 2001. The U. S. Supreme Court decided the election on December 12, 2000, because it claimed there was not sufficient time for Florida to submit its slate of electors before January 6, 2001. This was absurd on its face. Detailed information on this case can be seen at: http://supct.law.cornell.edu/supct/html/00-949.ZPC.html and http://www.censurethefive.org/.

Americans paid dearly for this decision of the U. S. Supreme Court to appoint George Bush President of the U. S. He gave us two lengthy and unresolved wars that are costly and bloody. He let New Orleans be destroyed by Hurricane Katrina, and failed to give rapid relief to its citizens. His policies sent our economy into depression. He nationalized the banks, furthering our country into socialism. He denied trials and *habeas corpus* to prisoners. He introduced torture as a means to obtain information. Some of those tortured were completely innocent, and some were tortured for fun. He spied on the public through the National Security Agency (NSA) surveillance satellite program.

Gonzales v. Raich (previously Ashcroft v. Raich), 545 U. S. 1 (2005), was a case in which the United States Supreme Court ruled on June 6, 2005 that under the Commerce Clause of the United States Constitution, which allows the United States Congress "To regulate Commerce...among the several States," Congress may ban the use of cannabis even where states approve its use for medicinal purposes. See http://en.wikipedia.org/wiki/Gonzales_v._Raich and http://www.alternet.org/story/14973/?page=2 for details.

Justice Thomas wrote a dissent, stating in part: "Respondent's local cultivation and consumption of marijuana is not "Commerce ... among the several States." "Certainly no evidence from the founding suggests that "commerce" included the mere possession of a good or some personal activity that did not involve trade or exchange for value. In the early days of the Republic, it would have been unthinkable that Congress could prohibit the local cultivation, possession, and consumption of marijuana." In fact, George Washington grew marijuana on his farm (my comment).

It is illegal in the United States to use certain medicines to treat ailments.

On August 19, 2009, p. A26, an editorial in the New York Times reported that the U. S. Supreme Court decided to review the conviction of Troy Davis for murder that current evidence shows that he did not commit. In dissent, Judges Scalia and Thomas argued that federal law prevents the courts from intervening on behalf of a death row inmate who claims to have proof of his own innocence. I assert that anyone under oath who refers to these individuals by their title of "Justice" is committing perjury.

D. COUNSEL OF YOUR OWN CHOOSING

Amendment VI to the U. S. Constitution says in part: 'In all criminal prosecutions, the accused shall.... have the assistance of counsel for his defense." The courts only permit attorneys sanctioned by the state, or the Defendant himself, to act as counsel. Nowhere in this Amendment does it require counsel to be a lackey of the Court. In some cases, it would be better to have a well informed non-attorney as counsel.

The primary obligation of an attorney should be to his or her client. However it often is not, especially if the attorney is court appointed. The attorney is always obligated to the judge in some way. If he angers or crosses the judge, this could have an effect in future cases. The same applies to his relationship with the prosecuting attorney. Thus an attorney may avoid certain strategies, such as jury nullification, particularly if they conflict with the judge's view of the law. Court appointed attorneys are known to be ill-prepared for trial, or even to be drunk or asleep during trials. They rarely do complete pretrial investigations.

E. RECOMMENDATIONS

"Prudence, indeed, will dictate that Governments long established, should not be changed for light and transient Causes...But, when a long Train of Abuses and Usurpations, pursuing invariably the same Object, evinces a Design to reduce them under absolute Despotism, it is [the people's] Right, it is their Duty, to throw off such Government, and to provide new Guards for their future Security." (U. S. Declaration of Independence, 1776).

Our country is doomed if we continue on the current path. What is the solution? Thomas Jefferson in 1787 reminded us that: " The tree of liberty must be refreshed from time to time with the blood of patriots and tyrants. It is its natural manure." Armed rebellion is a tempting thought. But Jefferson also reminded us that a revolution would be needed every 30 years as a new generation would be the rulers. This is too bloody and expensive a solution to be viable.

The ultimate culprits in our demise are the people themselves. They elect the rascals to public office. Their recklessness must be curbed. My suggestion is to require the passing of a comprehensive test on the U. S. Constitution and the voter's state constitution as a requirement to vote or to serve in public office. The voter and candidates must also swear, under penalty of law, to uphold these constitutions.

The test must not be administered by a government agency. There is too much danger of fraud. The test and qualification must be given by private organizations whose purpose is to support constitutional governments. The two organizations that immediately come to mind are the American Civil Liberties Union (ACLU) and the CATO Institute. They can give the tests together or they can operate separately and each give the tests in alternate years.

The ACLU is considered to be a wild left-wing organization, and the Cato Institute is considered to be a wild right-wing organization. Both of these characterizations are incorrect. Both organizations are middle of the road, in that they both want to preserve the country as it was intended and should be: a constitutional republic. The real radicals are in the so-called mainstream. These are the ignorant voters who have destroyed freedom in our country. If they do not understand and support constitutional government, they should not be allowed to vote or serve.

Every year at the Passover meal, Jews read and discuss the exodus from Egypt. Over 90% of American Jews attend this event every year. That is why the Jews never forgot who they are and what they should be, even though they have a 3700 year history. If all Americans would read the U. S. Constitution from cover to cover every year at the Independence Day picnic, we too would remember who we should be and, hopefully, behave accordingly. It would also help if every year, Justices of the U. S. Supreme Court led discussions with constitutional experts on national TV. Perhaps the Justices would also learn what this country is supposed to be.

THE LAW IS MEANT TO PROTECT THE PEOPLE; BUT, AS IT PROPAGATES, IT ENSLAVES THEM

THE AMOUNT OF JUSTICE IS INVERSELY RELATED TO THE NUMBER OF LAWS

Printed in Dunstable, United Kingdom

91226248R00147